Duck Soup for the Soul

The way of Living Louder & Laughing Longer

by Swami Beyondananda

To Henning
May the FARCE be with you!

Hysteria Publications
A Division of Sourcebooks, Inc.
Naperville, IL • Bridgeport, CT

Cover Design: Eric M. O'Malley, Sourcebooks, Inc.

Published by Sourcebooks, Inc.
Naperville Office
P.O. Box 372
Naperville, IL 60566
630-961-3900
Fax: 630-961-2168

Bridgeport Office
P.O. Box 38581
Bridgeport, CT 06605
203-333-9399
Fax: 203-367-7188

ISBN 1-887166-28-9

Printed and bound in the United States of America

10 9 8 7 6 5 4 3 2 1

To my wife, Trudy, who has been cooking Duck Soup in our household ever since we met, and whose playfulness, kindness, and good humor remind me to live what I'm writing about.

Acknowledgments

I would first like to acknowledge Deb Werksman for her unwavering faith in this project and her belief in the Swami (not as a religious figure, but as a successful author). I would like to thank Deb and editor Lysbeth Guillorn for their constructive feedback and editing. I would also like to acknowledge those creative thinkers out there who always remember to send me interesting names: my aunt Sonia Bhaerman, and friends Janet Williams, Dave Sternfeld, and Charley Thweatt. I'd also like to thank my friend Caroline Casey for always acknowledging the Swami when she quotes him, and for letting the Swami borrow her own marvelous vision of transformational art that causes institutions to crumble while people are left standing. Finally, I want to thank my wife, Trudy, who remained steadfast and cheery while I scaled the creative heights of ecstasy, and the creative depths of, if not Hell, then certainly Heck.

“To be happy in life, you must be able to take a joke. And if you can leave a few also, that’s even better.”

–Harry Cohen Baba

Table of Contents

Table of Contents

Preface:

Life Is Duck Soup... And we Are The Laughingstock

I have some shocking news. Are you sitting down? Okay, here goes. Life may actually be easier than we think. I can already hear you protesting that life is hardly easy. And I agree that life can easily be hard. But what if I told you that there is a way that life can easily be easy, and hardly be hard at all? What if I told you that rather than being a do-or-die ordeal, life can be "Duck Soup?"

I know what you are thinking. The Swami must be high on quack. After all, life is fraught with adversity, is it not? And that is true. But thanks to a close encounter with a great Fu Ling master, I now see how wholehearted laughter can reverse the adverse effects of adversity–and turn any stew into Duck Soup.

Duck Soup is similar to chicken soup in its healing powers. The only difference is, you don't need a chicken to make Duck Soup–or, for that matter, a duck. You are the main ingredient in Duck Soup, which is made primarily from your own laughingstock. Each time you laugh, you add to the laughingstock. Now we all know that life can feel like a pressure cooker nowadays. A good guffaw can take the pressure off–and that sure beats blowing your lid. When you bubble over with laughter and everything feels just ducky, you've got Duck Soup.

No doubt about it. Laughter makes life easier. But don't take my word for it. Four out of five metaphysicians recommend levity as the best way to rise above whatever is bringing you down. And humorologists tell us that the mirth found in the average one liner (about one youngman of laughter) is enough to release a megahurt of emotional pain.

Am I serious? Absolutely not. But I used to be. It has been said that there is a seeker born every minute, and two to take him along the path–and I started out as a seeker of truth and wisdom. I had read every spiritual tract imaginable until the day Harry Cohen Baba, master of the Zen Cohen, slipped me an epigram that stopped me in my tracts. And in a flash of enlightening, I became fooly-realized. I realized that I was a fool and there was nothing I could do about it but laugh. And since that time, I have dedicated myself to increasing the laugh-force on the planet and helping others attain fool-realization.

Harry Cohen Baba dubbed me the Guru of Ho-ho-holy Hee-hee-healing, and gave me his recipe for Duck Soup, which I pass on to you. In this book, you will learn how the daily practice of Fu Ling can help you make a hearty laughingstock from your own ingredients. You will learn some simple tips for maintaining jestive health, and for finding your vehicle to bring Duck Soup to others. Finally, you will learn to extract spiritual nourishment not just from our sacred cows, but from the bull as well. I cannot guarantee that you will achieve your fool potential. That is up to you. But if you do your Omwork Assignments at the end of each chapter, you will activate your laugh force and very likely increase your laugh-expectancy.

May this book help you live fooly and laugh heartily. May you wake up laughing and leave laughter in your wake. And may the Farce be with you.

Swami Beyondananda

Introduction:

How Swami Got Struck By Enlightening and Became Fooly-Realized

Like many experiences of enlightenment, my awakening came in the wake of a dark night of the soul. I had moved to New York to study Dowism with the noted stock market guru Yuan Tibet. I religiously followed his investment advice, putting my life savings into an anti-aging product made from the gallbladder of an African antelope–"gnu bile" it was called. It was being marketed as Ch'i Whiz, the first Chinese herbal preparation that could be spread on crackers. Initial tests showed conclusively that the formula indeed made subjects twenty years younger. I sat back and eagerly awaited the riches to begin rolling in. But the product's fabulous effectiveness turned out to be its downfall. The FDA pulled it off the shelves after a teenager took it and disappeared.

I frantically tried to call Yuan Tibet for his sage advice, but he could not be found. Tragically, there had been some prophet-taking on Wall Street, somebody took him, and he was never heard from again. My whole world had come crashing down on me in one swell poop, and I found myself in the middle of a near-debt experience. Not only was I a fiscal wreck, but an emotional wreck as well. As is often the case following a serious karma crash, I sought meaning in the tragedy. I cannot tell you how many days I spent shaking my fist at the sky and demanding, "What is the MEANING of this?"

I knew something needed to change, and I began looking for a sign. At first, I just saw the usual signs. "Stop." "Yield." "No loitering." But one day soon after, I was riding the subway and there amidst all of the other ads was the sign I was looking for:

Harry Cohen Baba
The Garment Center Saint
"We specialize in alterations."

I'd already heard of Harry Cohen Baba. As the story goes, he was born into a family of tailors on New York's Lower East Side and at a very early age demonstrated remarkable healing powers. Whenever an item of torn or frayed clothing was brought into his presence, he would wave his hand over the garment, say a few loving words like "Pull yourself together," or "Don't be frayed," and magically the garment would be healed. For many years he owned a tailor shop, where he toiled needlelessly.

As word of the Garment Center Saint's talent for healing spread, people began coming to him to mend not just their garments but the very fabric of their lives. Many of those who came were misfits whose habits left them poorly suited for life. Others were hanging on by a thread. Their entire material existence needed altering. But Harry was afraid he couldn't measure up. One night, weary from wrestling with this challenge, he was visited in a dream by a strange apparition. Wearing a long white beard and dressed in a caftan, the figure identified himself as Yeshivananda, leader of an obscure sect known as Men of the Cloth. He told Harry that his purpose in life was to use the spiritual to heal the material through the magic of laughter. "You're going to need better material, though," Yeshivananda told him. "You must go to the mountains and sit at the feet of the great Fu Ling masters."

As a newly-ordained Man of the Cloth, Harry Cohen Baba made his first of many journeys to the mountains, where he sat with every great Fu Ling master who ever held an audience. He sat with Benny, he sat with Henny–and yes, he even sat with Lenny. From them he learned the Zen Cohen, a configuration of words designed to ignite a moment of enlightenment with a spark of laughter. He became a tailor of tales, gathering the finest material and weaving it into a piece that would suit anyone in need of alterations.

And so it was with great anticipation that I signed up to accompany the Garment Center Saint on one of his New Deli pilgrimages. A new deli had just opened on 37th Street, and Harry Cohen Baba was going to check it out. I sat reverently in the great one's presence as he devoured a pastrami sandwich and washed it down with Dr. Brown's Cel-Ray Tonic. Finally, I could contain myself no longer. "Oh, Garment Centered One," I blurted out, "what is the secret of happiness?"

"Digesting," he said, his mouth full, barely looking up from the plate.

"That's it? Just sitting here and eating food is the secret of happiness?" I asked, greatly disappointed.

"Who said anything about food?" he replied. "I said the secret of happiness is die-jesting. We all gotta die someday, so we might as well die jesting. And since you never really know when the grin reaper may show up, I suggest you start jesting now."

"How do I do that?" I wanted to know.

"Well," said Harry Cohen Baba, finally looking up from his sandwich, "do you ever wake up in the morning with a funny feeling?"

"Yes!" I answered excitedly. "All the time."

"Well, there you are," he said. "You got a head start. Just go with it."

"But Garment Centered One," I protested, "you don't understand. Everything that has happened to me in the past few months has left me bitter and angry. I don't feel like laughing."

"Of course you don't," he said sympathetically. "That's because you have taken things poisonally. But I guarantee it. You get off those sour grapes and onto a diet of Snickers and Chuckles, and your life will become Duck Soup."

The only association I had with Duck Soup was the Marx Brothers movie.

"Do you mean that life will become a funny movie?" I asked.

"It already is a funny movie," he explained. "The

difference is, you will be able to hear the laugh track. But there is another meaning for Duck Soup that goes back to when I was a little boy. Duck Soup means 'piece of cake.'"

"You mean that life is sweet icing on the top with lots of empty calories on the bottom?" I asked, puzzled.

"No, shmendrick! It means that life is really easier than we think it is."

"That's easy for you to say," I grumbled, "but I just don't see it. How is life so easy?"

Harry Cohen Baba sighed. "OK, OK. You want to know the real secret of happiness? So I'll tell you. A man goes to the doctor and says, 'Doctor, it hurts when I do this.' And the doctor says, 'So don't do this.'"

I reacted to this Zen Cohen with such an explosion of laughter that the other deli customers stopped eating to watch. A concerned physician came over to see if I was suffering from the involuntary gag response. Harry Cohen Baba assured him that I was fine, but the doctor did hang around to make sure I didn't upchuckle. To make a long satori short, this was how I got struck by enlightening and achieved fool-realization. My clown chakra opened, and it made me see funny. And the funniest thing I saw was me. Here I was, trying to achieve happiness by doing this, that, and the other thing–and trying to outdo myself had just about done me in. It turns out that all I needed to feel happy was to laugh heartily.

When the initial wave of laughter subsided, the first thing I uttered was a spontaneous answer to the Zen Cohen that had enlightened me: "Doctor, it HELPS when I do this!" And I collapsed into uncontrollable laughter again.

For the next week, I was high on levity, wandering around in state of euphoria, telling every stranger I saw the same Zen Cohen: "Doctor, it hurts when I do this."

"So don't do this."

Needless to say, I wanted to be able to have Duck Soup all the time. So I asked Harry Cohen Baba for the recipe.

"OK," he said. "I'll boil it down for you. I will teach you the Way of the Fu Ling Master, that which has been called the Four-Fold Path."

Introduction

I was an eager student full of questions. "Why the Four-Fold Path?"

"Listen," he said, "I've been a tailor all my life, so you can take my word for it. Any more than four folds, it gets sloppy. But if you follow this Four-Fold Path, everything will be ducky."

Whereupon the Great One laid out the Four-Fold Path before me. "First step," he told me, "is you must practice FUNdamentalism, accent on 'fun'–not to be confused with FundaMENTALism, which emphasizes the 'mental.'

"The second thing," he continued, "is to release those jestive blockages. We've been given the marvelous human jestive system to help turn the material of life into laughter. You can't expect to be happy if you suffer from hindered-jestion.

"Next, you must learn to drive your karma and curb your dogma." I must have looked perplexed, because he explained, "In other words, life is a joyride when you find your expressway for bringing happiness to the world, and you feel safe enough to leave your pet beliefs at home.

"Finally," he proclaimed, "if you are to become a Fu Ling Master yourself, you must milk the sacred cow, and take the bull by the horns. You must find the things in life that bring true joy and nourishment–and learn to laugh at the bull."

For two years, I studied and practiced the Way of the Fu Ling Master, until one day Harry Cohen Baba beckoned me into his presence. "You have studied well, and now it is time for you to go."

I was shocked. "Go where? I don't want to go."

"But you must," he replied gently. "I am growing weary and soon will no longer have the strength to spin another yarn. You have mastered the Zen Cohen, but are woefully deficient in wordplay. Therefore, I am sending you to India to study in the Punjab." And so I sadly left. My studies went well, as I learned to hurl pun-jabs and trade jibes with the best of them. When my time was up, I returned home and was saddened to find that my beloved Harry Cohen Baba was on the verge of taking his final samadhi and leaving the physical plane.

"Don't leave, don't leave!" I protested.

He quieted me with a wave of his hand. "It is time for me to leave the material existence," he said softly.

"But why? Why?" I asked.

"Because, *boychick*, I have run out of material."

He reached into his nightstand drawer and pulled out a dog-eared baseball card from the 1950s. It was then that I realized the Mantle was being passed on to me. Placing it gently in my hand, he said, "I now dub you the Guru of Ho-ho-holy Hee-hee-healing."

"But," I protested. "You're the guru, not me."

"We're all gurus," he insisted. "Listen, I'll spell it out for you. G-U-R-U. Gee, you are you. The true guru has fun being himself–and gives others permission to do the same. So I give you permission. Now go and have fun!"

With that, he poked his finger in my third eye, Three Stooges style, and I could feel the surge of his remaining laugh force entering my being. And he offered a final blessing: "May you help everyone you meet milk the sacred cow for all it's worth, and turn the bull into laughingstock."

As Harry Cohen Baba's soul prepared to take flight, his weakened jestive system offered up one more quip: "Everybody needs samadhi sometime." And as the last word of the joke escaped, so did his last breath. Like the realized Fu Ling Masters before him, he managed to Die-Jest the last moment of life.

And so he left me to carry on. Which explains all the carrying-on I've been doing all these years. And which also explains this book. For truly I have been on a steady diet of Duck Soup since my master departed. My life has gotten funnier, and believe me, life is easier when it's funny. I owe it all to the Four-Fold Path, which I unfold now before you.

I trust you to fold it back up when you are done.

Part I

Practice FUNdamentalism: Accent on "FUN"

The FUNdamentalist Revival

As anyone who switches on the 6:00 P.M. news can see, the world is in a grave state. That is the bad news. The good news is, the best way to overcome all this gravity is with levity. It is not surprising then, that in these times of great upheaval–not to mention downheaval–more and more people are turning to FUNdamentalism–accent on "fun."

We FUNdamentalists believe that life is a joke, but God is laughing with us, not at us. We believe that fun is FUNdamental, that beneath all of the stress, distress, and negativity we see around us, there is a deep well of joy that is the source of deep wellness. We believe that by surrendering to the Farce and by playing to God every day, we can open our clown chakra and actually hear the laugh track. We embrace the material world as a source of great material which will keep us and God laughing long after the final credits roll. And we play for Nonjudgment Day, the glorious moment when the laugh track becomes audible to all and we finally get the joke.

Yes, a FUNdamentalist revival is in full swing as weary seekers return to the real old time religion where the fun comes before the mental and celebration outweighs cerebration. We FUNdamentalists realize that Nonjudgment Day is at hand, and the best way to illuminate the darkness is to make light of it. And miracles are occurring daily! Not only are practicing FUNdamentalists finding their laugh-force revitalized, but they are reporting that chronic jestive disorders such as irregularhilarity, irony deficiency, humorrhoids, and even truth decay are clearing up as if by magic. Some have taken a vow of levity and embarked upon the path of the Fu Ling master. You may have already encountered Fu Ling acolytes going door-to-door collecting jokes for the humorless, or holding Fun Raisers to increase the laugh-expectancy on the planet. And a few fortunate souls have already achieved the FUNdamentalist ideal of "die-jesting" where they leave 'em laughing and go out on a "ha" breath. But you need not die to get the joke. Millions of formerly unhappy souls are experiencing hours of atfunment and enjoyousness as they remember and practice the five tenets of FUNdamentalism that have been passed down to us from the ancient Fu Ling Masters:

The FUNdamentalist Humanifesto

1. Life Is a Joke, But God Is Laughing With Us Not at Us
2. Fun Is Fundamental
3. A Laugh Track Has Been Provided
4. The Reason We Are Put in the Material World Is to Get More Material
5. Nonjudgment Day Is at Hand

Life Is a Joke–But God Is Laughing with Us, Not at Us

Ever since that moment of awakening when the first primeval soul looked up to the heavens with wonder–and a bird splatted him right in the third eye–we human beings have been seeking the meaning of life. Some mystics–pessimystics they are called–insist that life is perpetual suffering and disappointment. These mystics can be heard today telling anyone who will listen that the sky is falling. Optimystics on the other hand see even the most depressing situation in a positive light. "The sky isn't falling," say the optimystics. "It just looks that way because we are ascending."

Still others insist that life is a test, and they spend a lifetime–not to mention all of their money–trying to find someone who has the Cliff's Notes. But as a FUNdamentalist, I have to believe that life is a joke. Now you are probably saying, "OK, I am waiting for the punchline." And that is precisely my point. We all are. That is why it is so ridiculous to be worrying about life being some kind of test. When we get the joke, we pass. And believe me, everyone passes.

Well, you might ask, how do I know that life is a joke? To be truthful, I do not actually know for certain. In fact, the only thing certain in life is uncertainty–and come to think of it, I'm not even sure about that. But the evidence is overwhelming. For one thing, many of those who have undergone "near-death experiences" have returned to life and reported "hearing the laugh track." When one is struck by enlightening like this, the clown chakra may be permanently opened. These fortunate souls are able to see farce-fields around people, and can accurately predict who will get a pie in the face and who will do the pie-throwing.

If third-hand anecdotal evidence doesn't do it for you, perhaps second-hand anecdotal evidence will. Let me tell you a true story that will lay to rest any doubts about the Creator's sense of humor. I live in the Texas Hill Country on a spread called the Cattlelack Ranch. Despite our deficiency in cattle, there is no scarcity of raccoons, whom I have found to be lifelong criminals without a smidgen of remorse. I must admit that when the most recent pack of raccoons decimated the garden, the thought crossed my mind that all of the Swami's disciples would look terrific in Davy Crockett hats.

But being a humane kind of guy, I went to the Humane Society and picked up several live traps. The man there instructed me to capture the animals live, then drop them off in the woods about fifteen miles away. This I did, and just as I was pulling into my driveway, I saw someone else–with similarly humane intentions–dropping off a family of raccoons on my land.

No doubt about it, God is a prankster Supreme and that was one of His milder practical jokes. For such an evolved Being, God's humor can sometimes be surprisingly physical-like volcanic lava rolling down a mountain towards a village below. Talk about a hotfoot. Whew. How about tectonic plates moving and a chunk of California falling off into the Pacific? Oops, that Wild and Crazy Guy just short-sheeted your bed. But He can be subtle, too. Like the First Law of Spermodynamics which states that those people who want to get pregnant will find it nearly impossible, while those trying to avoid it will hit the jackpot every time. Believe me, every one of those Murphy's Laws was hand-written by the Creator Himself. Remember that movie back in the '70s where God is modeled after George Burns? In actuality, George Burns was modeled after God.

Now I do not in any way want to leave the impression that we humans are merely the butt of a crude joke. While it is true that God stays up most nights watching us on the Comedy Channel, believe me when I tell you that God is laughing with us, not at us. You cannot imagine how much pleasure it gives Him to watch us in what Harry Cohen Baba used to call "the *shlemiel-shlemazel* waltz." The *shlemiel*, or Happy Fool, is the clumsy oaf who is always spilling soup on someone. The *shlemazel*, or Sad Clown, is the ill-fated recipient of spilled soup. As those aforementioned "farce fields" reform and realign, we take turns being *shlemiel* and *shlemazel*, so we get the fool spectrum of experience. And each of us gets ample opportunity to be a straight man for one of these cosmic jests. It's like jury duty. No one is exempt. Can a gay woman be a straight man? Absolutely. It happens every day.

If life is nothing but a joke, you might ask, then what is the purpose of free will? I will tell you. We get to choose whether or not we laugh.

While we FUNdamentalists are ardent pro-laughers, we are pro-choice as well. We honor each other's right to not be amused. Our failure to laugh in no way spoils God's fun. But I figure, why resist a Farce that is greater than any of us? If life is a sitcom, why not sit calm and enjoy it?

Fun Is FUNdamental

Fundamentally, FUNdamentalists believe that fun is fundamental. In fact, we say fun is the fundament upon which the entire world sits. Underneath all that sadness, fear, anger, greed, and all the other human muck and mire, there is an infinite well of joy. When we drink from this well through wholehearted laughter, we are injesting 100 percent Spirit, made from concentrate. Unfortunately, this deep well of joy–the source of deep wellness-is largely untapped. And it isn't just us FUNdamentalists saying this. Secular humorists at the forefront of the humor potential movement agree that we use only a small portion of our potential to enjoy ourselves, and use even a smaller fraction of our ability to humor others.

This may come as a surprise, particularly when you look at your Ascended Mastercard statement and see how much you spent this past year pursuing fun. It is a buyological fact that in our consumer-oriented society people are encouraged to spend all the money they have-or more, if they can swing it–to buy anything and everything they think they need to make them happy.

But just because fun is purchased and consumed in large quantities, doesn't mean it is actually enjoyed. In fact, genuine enjoyment-or enjoyousness, as we FUNdamentalists call it-is about as rare nowadays as a zero balance on a credit card account. Now I don't want to place any blame here (as a FUNdamentalist working for Nonjudgment Day I believe people who blame are the cause of all the world's problems) but I cannot help but notice how dysFUNsional spiritual beliefs make people feel they don't deserve to enjoy life. How about the idea that we are conceived in sin, and if we do not carefully dot every "i" and cross every "t" we are condemned to an eternal weenie roast-with us as the weenie? Welcome to the world, little fella.

So prodded on by what the Freudians would call "happiness envy," we blindly seek feelfullment, but never find fulfillment because deep down we believe that feeling good is bad. Fortunately, there is a way out. In order to enjoy fun, you must practice enjoying not having fun. This is easier than you might imagine. First of all, in the course of the average day, you will encounter numerous situations that are not intrinsically enjoyable. (If this is not the case, you should be writing this book instead of reading it.) Second of all, if you miss enjoying the unenjoyable today, you will get another chance tomorrow, and even more chances the next day. So if you fail to enjoy your misery, it won't be for lack of opportunity.

If this seems like a daunting task, take heart. It may help you to realize that you already enjoy not enjoying things more than you imagine. Harry Cohen Baba was a great teacher in this regard. One day, he challenged me to find the loophole in the Golden Rule. I puzzled over it for days, and even called an attorney friend whose specialty was Universal Law and still I couldn't solve the puzzle. "OK," I finally told him. "I give up. What is the loophole in the Golden Rule?"

"Sadists and masochists," he replied. "If a masochist does unto someone else the way he wants to be done unto, doesn't that make him a sadist? Conversely, a true sadist would be kind to a masochist so as to deny him the pleasure of pain." I couldn't argue with that logic. I realized that the reason why the Golden Rule is widely preached but rarely practiced is because so many of us human beings have learned to get pleasure out of pain–and we don't even realize it. So the next logical step is to consciously enjoy the pleasure you get from suffering.

One of the most remarkable things about Harry Cohen Baba was his ability to totally delight in not having fun. I never met anyone who got such pleasure out of not enjoying himself. He used to love going to a deli over on 43rd Street because the food was so terrible. "I enjoy a lousy meal every now and then," he used to tell me. "First of all, it makes me really appreciate a good meal. Secondly, I get great pleasure out of complaining."

How many times has someone asked you how you're doing and you replied, "I can't complain." That is not true. You can complain! In fact, I insist that you complain, and complain as long and as loudly as you like–as long as you promise to enjoy every minute of it. This practice, which the Fu Ling masters called "atfunment," is one of the keys to mastering FUNdamentalism. That is when you ask yourself, "How would this feel if I pretended it was fun?" When you realize you are enjoying yourself pretending it is fun, you have achieved a moment of atfunment. These feelings of atfunment will help you turn whatever "soup" you find yourself in into Duck Soup.

A Laugh Track Has Been Provided

The FUNdamentalist scriptures tell us that on the Eighth Day, God saw that the world was funny and created laughter. He's been enjoying the show ever since. And He figured, since we were humoring Him, He would humor us. So He gave us the gift of laughter so that we could see the world from His perspective. Because to God, it's all a joke. What does He care? Does God have to get up every morning and go to work? No, His work is done. He's only worked one week in the entire history of existence! Those people who insist God is dead, they are wrong. He's retired. He turned the whole Business over to His Son about 2,000 years ago. And if I'm not mistaken, that means we own a share.

Being retired, the Creator has nothing to do but sit around and be entertained by our antics. And because we FUNdamentalists value His gift of laughter so much, we want to humor Him just as He has humored us. That is why the devout FUNdamentalist stops all other activities to play several times a day. This devotional state of playing to God means surrendering to the Farce and offering oneself up as entertainment. This is not a purely altruistic activity, however. There's an old saying that idle hands do the devil's work, and God is no exception. Being retired and having all that time on His hands, He has little else to do but think up practical jokes all day. FUNdamentalists believe that God is less likely to impose His brand of amusement on those busy amusing themselves. Which is why we FUNdamentalists play with each other all the time. It is during these moments of fervently playing that FUNdamentalists have been able to feel the levitational pull to counteract all of the gravity in life, and have been able to see things from the Creator's La-Z-Boy right in front of that big screen TV–and clearly hear the laugh track.

But playing isn't only to humor God. When we get together with other folks at those FUNdamentalist revivals I mentioned earlier, we get so caught up in playing that we forget we are doing it for God's amusement, and we begin playing for our own salvation. And as we FUNdamentalists say, a family that plays together stays together. The latest scientific studies say that children who grow up in families that play regularly show far less truth decay than children growing up in dysFUNsional families–and are less likely to become assaholics or whinos in later life.

FUNdamentalists know for certain that the laugh track is out there, but even the most ardent FUNdamentalist will sometimes get off track. While we recommend farce-feeding only for the most stubborn case of humorrhoids, a gentle laughsitive will often be just as effective. In fact, canned laughter is now sold over-the-counter at most large drug stores, and we recommend that every FUNdamentalist household have some on hand in the medicine cabinet. At the first sign of irregularhilarity, I suggest you open the can of laughter and let it fill the room. Then recite each of your worries, concerns and troubles. After each one, turn the laughter up until you join in laughing yourself. Repeat as often as necessary, and it is inevitable that you will get back on the laugh track once again.

The Reason we Are in the Material world Is to Get More Material

Anyone who watches the show and listens to the laugh track for any length of time comes to realize that we are put in the material world to get more material. Why else would we be here? The FUNdamentalist scriptures say that once upon a time, God didn't have any body. So He created us. It is a scientific fact: because laughter is a physiological activity, having physiology is necessary in order to laugh. Spirit is immaterial, so it has to materialize in order to experience anything–which explains this material existence. Without the material, there would be nothing to laugh about, and no one to do the laughing. We humans are doing double duty for the Creator. Not only are we the show, but we are the audience as well. We embody laughter, and so God is able to laugh.

Yeshivananda, that great Man of the Cloth, lived to a ripe old age, so ripe that he was beginning to ferment. A disciple of his asked him, "Master, you clearly can ascend any time you want. You made your last karma payment years ago, and I'm sure you have enough good deeds stashed in that Swiss bank account of yours to last you another millennium. Why do you stay on the material plane?"

"Are you crazy?" he retorted. "Only in the material world could I get such fabulous material! Later on, after the show, I'll have a glass of tea, and then I'll ascend."

The FUNdamentalist uses material to get to the spiritual, and uses the spiritual to heal the material. A case in point is the aforementioned Men of the Cloth sect which originated in the Jewish ghetto in Eastern Europe in the late 19th Century during the now-famous "chicken blight." With local poultry ravaged by disease, Jewish mothers could no longer prepare their fabled chicken soup. A delegation of townspeople approached Yeshivananda, who was known for his wit and wisdom, with their dilemma. "Well, then," he told them, "make Duck Soup instead."

"But we've never made Duck Soup," protested one of the afflicted chicken flickers. "And besides, there are no ducks either!"

"How very fortunate," replied Yeshivananda.

"Fortunate? What's so fortunate?" demanded one of the villagers.

"Since you've never made Duck Soup," Yeshivananda replied, "no one has ever tasted it. Therefore, no one will notice the duck is missing."

This made perfect sense to the townsfolk, but then

another objection was raised. "What about the healing power of chicken soup? How much healing can a non-existent duck offer?"

"Oh," said Yeshivananda, "its healing power is infinitely greater than chicken soup."

"And how is that?" asked one man skeptically.

"Very simple," replied the wise one. "Can an invisible duck be measured?"

"Of course not!" answered the man.

"Well then," Yeshivananda pronounced, "the healing power of Duck Soup is immeasurable!"

And so it was that Duck Soup became a staple of the local diet. True to Yeshivananda's words, the laughter that resulted from re-telling this tale provided far more spiritual nourishment than chicken soup ever had. Encouraged by the way laughter brightened their days, the Men of the Cloth (as they came to call themselves) began bringing comedy to the tailor shops where many toiled. Since there was no place for non-workers to sit down in these sweat shops, stand-up was born. And since no one could afford good material, the Men of the Cloth used scraps from their own lives to fabricate their routines, weaving material into humorous, healing stories to make others laugh.

"Even the best material gets worn out after a while," Harry Cohen Baba used to say, "so somebody has to keep spinning new yarns."

This is especially true if we see that rise in laugh-expectancy they are predicting. Researchers at the Center for the Study of Jestive Disorders in Pratt Falls, New York, tell us that the average human being can now expect to laugh ten thousand more times over the course of a lifetime than his or her parents did. While Comedy Factories will undoubtedly proliferate, we FUNdamentalists consider it our laugh purpose to contribute as much good material as we can.

This is easier than you can imagine. As we FUNdamentalists say, "Material happens." So remember, when things go wrong, it's all material. Even the worst time might end up being great material. This is good news. It means that regardless of what your bank account is, you can create material success! Because if your laugh story can make someone chuckle, you've added to the laughingstock. And even if you live a routine existence, why shouldn't it be a great routine? As Harry Cohen Baba used to say, "The first requirement for a healthy human being is, you gotta be able to take a joke. And if you can leave a few as well, all the better."

Nonjudgment Day Is at Hand

Nonjudgment Day is what we FUNdamentalists have been fervently and joyously playing for. When enough people choose laughing instead of condemning we will reach uncritical mass. On Nonjudgment Day, the Laugh Force will become so powerful that the laugh track becomes audible, and farce-fields are clearly visible. On Nonjudgment Day, everyone will win beauty contests. Folks will gather in public esteem baths where they will bathe unashamed in unconditional love. Lawyers will disappear, and all our trials will be over. Soldiers everywhere will lay down their arms. They will look very funny with their arms down on the ground and their butts sticking up in the air, but the world will be a safer place because you cannot attack anybody in this position (unless, of course, you have just had burritos and are adept at gastral projection).

This will be celebrated as Disarmaggedon, and will be the end of the human race as we know it. We will realize that life isn't a race, so we can stop running. On Nonjudgment Day, all those people who have been running a little behind for so many years will finally get caught up. They will take a deep breath, stop running their little behinds off, and sit calm. There they will find that whatever they have been chasing is already patiently waiting for them.

Regardless of how or when the world ends up, each of us must individually face Nonjudgment. God or one of His assistants will switch on the VCR (if you're lucky you'll get Ralph Edwards from that old "This Is Your Life" TV show), and you'll see an entire lifetime of outtakes–all of those embarrassing moments, those times when you tried with all your might to look good and looked foolish instead, and all of those other Larry, Moe, or Curly moments when you were a stooge for God. Your intake of these outtakes will be made easier by the fact that you will be hearing the full audience laugh track as you watch your shenanigans. It is usually during this process that enlightening strikes and you achieve fool realization.

Yes, Nonjudgment Day is near. How quickly it comes about depends on the quality of the material we create and extract from the material world. God is the Sponsor of this long-running situation comedy, and our Universe is the Network. But we write the scripts and perform the "schtick" ourselves. As we learn to heal our jestive blockages, drive our karma, curb our dogma, milk those sacred cows, and take the bull by the horns, the quality of the programming is bound to improve.

A Zen Cohen

After one of his talks, Harry Cohen Baba was asked by a student, "Don't you think it is a bit presumptuous to think that we human beings actually deserve to enjoy life?" The Garment Center Saint offered the following parable: It was Yom Kippur, the Jewish Day of Atonement. The doctor, the lawyer, and the banker were all in the front row of the synagogue. As was the custom, each was beating his breast and declaring his unworthiness: "I'm unworthy! I'm unworthy! I'm unworthy!" Just then, the lowly janitor walked in. He observed the scene, and he too walked to the front and began crying out, "I'm unworthy! I'm unworthy! I'm unworthy!"

The lawyer turned to the banker and said, "So look who thinks he's unworthy?"

Any Questions?

Dear Swami:
I notice that you continually refer to God as a "He." Surely an enlightened male like yourself doesn't subscribe to the belief that our Creator is a man. A lot of feminists out here are pretty upset. How about it, Swami?

Lynne Schmob
Seattle, Washington

Dear Lynne:

Your point is well taken, so let me explain. Since God was the First Laugher and will no doubt be around to get the Last Laugh, I have always secretly referred to our Creator as the Ho-Ho-Holy Hee-Hee-Healer. I originally thought about shortening that to "Ho," but this would have been even more ripe for Ms.-interpretation. I decided to go with "Hee," which looks stupid, so it became "He." Hope this answers your question.

> Dear Swami:
>
> What is your theological position on chocolate? My minister tells me that chocolate is an insidious evil that causes addiction, dissolution, and decay. And yet, when I bite into a chunk of my favorite sweet treat, I am filled with such ecstatic delight that I know for certain God exists. Should I pursue the chocolate path or is the road to hell indeed paved with Chunkies?
>
> *Cara Zmatick*
> *Grand Rapids, Michigan*

Dear Cara:

It is true that some strict fundaMENTALists insist that chocolate is "the Devil's Food" and that the spiritually pure should only indulge in angelfood. Personally, I feel these people are just afraid to face the dark side. Actually, chocolate worship dates back to beginning of recorded history. According to those ancient scrolls, the Tut Sea Rolls, the Egyptians worshipped cocoa as the Supreme Bean and the first pyramids were pocket-sized and made of chocolate. Modern day chocolytes include the Goobers, who seek to experience Almond Joy by immersing themselves in vats of hot chocolate; the Raisinettes, who worship chocolate Santas mounted on their dashboards; and the Salivation Army, who selflessly distribute chocolate kisses to the homeless. I am all in favor of celebrating chocolate and other life pleasures as manifestations of Spirit. As we FUNdamentalists say, "Jesus savors!"

> Dear Swami:
> I've always been the worrying kind. You name it, I've lost sleep over it. Sure, I've worried about the usual stuff-school, money, relationships, health. But I worry about other things as well-like tidal waves. Now I live here in Oregon and there hasn't been a tidal wave here in all of recorded history-and that has me worried. It seems we're long overdue. Then there are those eerie mornings when I wake up without a care in the world. And that's when I really start to worry because I figure I'm gonna be socked with something so unimaginably bad that I haven't been able to think of it yet. Now don't get me wrong. It's not worrying that I mind. In fact, I kind of like it-gives me something to do. But I'm worried there might be something wrong with me for worrying so much. Any advice?
>
> *Klaus Trafobic*
> *Springfield, Oregon*

Dear Klaus:

Sounds like you need my Peaceful Worrier training, where you learn to worry to your heart's content–and never let it bother you. See, worrying should be no cause for concern. It's a natural human emotion. So relax. Ninety percent of the things you worry about will never happen anyway, and the 10 percent that does happen will keep you so busy, you won't have time to worry. That's why it's important to enjoy your worrying while you can.

In fact, your penchant for extended worry might even be considered a gift. Most people would give anything to have someone to do all their worrying for them. If you charged for this service, believe me, it would eliminate your money worries. I suggest you take on other people's worries, forget about your own, and make a comfortable living as a mercenary worrier.

> Dear Swami:
> I have heard many so-called "New Age" gurus insinuate that we are all manifestations of God. All of my prior religious training teaches that we human beings are sinners who can only be saved by God's grace. I just don't see how we imperfect humans can all of a sudden claim to be expressing God? This idea of human divinity is sacrilegious.
>
> *Misty Mark*
> *Charlotte, North Carolina*

Dear Misty:

You have reasoned yourself into what is known in theology as a "cul-de-sacrilege." And this is understandable because in spiritual matters, linear reasoning always ends up at a dead end. But if we try circular logic for a change, and view life as a wheel, with God as the hub and each of us as a spoke, it is easy to see how we are spokespersons for the Divine.

> Dear Swami:
> I know you're one of those Pollyanna positive thinking types and I have to tell you that the only true path through life is to accept and embrace the misery and tragedy. My secret for successful living is: Expect to be miserable! That way, if it happens, there's no surprise. And if it doesn't, well there's a brief respite. What do you think?
>
> *Israel Bummer*
> *Somerville, New Jersey*

Practice Fundamentalism: Accent on "Fun"

Dear Israel:

Hey, whatever makes you happy.

> Dear Swami:
> I know this has been asked a million times, but I've never received a satisfactory answer: Why do bad things happen to good people?
>
> *Ann Sadat*
> *Houston, Texas*

Dear Ann:

This is a question theologians have wrestled with for centuries, and just when it seems one has pinned it to the mat, that squirmy little guy always slips out of the full-Aquinas headlock and says, "OK, who's next?" One popular theory currently making the rounds maintains that good people aren't really that good, and bad things aren't that bad. According to this point of view, every basically good person has some kind of karmic skeleton in the closet–and if you take into account past lives, the chances of even a saint escaping the cosmic come-around is virtually nil. That's the bad news. The good news is that bad things are really good because they provide valuable lessons that help us grow. Do you follow this logic? I'm not sure I do. If it really were the case, you could expect to receive more calls from friends saying, "I'm so happy I could wet myself! I just broke my leg!" Likewise, lottery winners would be inconsolable. Can you just picture one being interviewed by reporters, sighing with deep sadness, "Well, I guess that's the end of my poverty lessons for a long, long time. What do I have to live for now?"

But I have a simpler explanation. Call it blind faith, call it informed belief, but I figure God must be dyslexic, and I let it go at that.

Swami's Omwork Assignment:

Have a Good Old-Fashioned FUNdamentalist Revival

Unlike other religions which designate a specific day of the week for devotion and worship, FUNdamentalists say that any day two or more gather together to laugh in God's name is a Ho-Ho-Holy Day. And when it comes to laughter, truly the more the merrier. There's nothing like a good, old-fashioned FUNdamentalist revival to revive the fun in your community. Here's the recipe:

Find a wide open space where anyone you know who shares your laugh-affirming values can gather under one big intent–to have fun.

Ask people to dress in their Funday finery-red noses, rubber ties, and oversized shoes are *de rigueur*, but it's fine to come disguised as normal people.

The ceremony generally begins with a reading from the Funday Sunnies–any book of jokes, quips, limericks, or puns will do–and then a rousing FUNdamentalist hymn like "Meet The Flintstones" to get everyone in the proper mood.

Our Golden Rule of Ho-ho-holy Hee-hee-healing is "Laugh thy neighbor as thyself," so spend the next part of the Revival looking at each other and laughing. Since so many of the great geniuses and innovators in our world were laughed at before they proved successful, it's only logical then, that facing laughter prepares us for success. And what better way to face laughter than to have others laugh in your face? To get the jestive juices flowing, many people will make funny faces. Others don't have to, since God has already done the job for them. Since we are all mirrors for each other, it doesn't matter whose face you are facing. When you reach the point where you realize you are laughing in your own face, you have achieved atfunment.

When the laughter dies down to a few snickers, giggles, and an occasional chuckle, and you have laughed yourselves into a peaceful bliss, it is time to pass the plate. FUNdamentalists often bring items to share from their own laughingstock–jokes, comedy CDs and videos, cartoons, books, and various jestive aids. The items are all put in one pile in the middle of the room, and everyone takes home a new fun item. Anything left over is donated to the humorless.

The Revival ends with the FUNdamentalist pledge: "All for fun and fun for all!" And everyone runs out to play until fundown.

Part II

Release Jestive Blockages

what is the Meaning of Laugh?

Ever since the first chuckle bubbled up the jestive tract and exploded into joyous laughter, we humans have been pondering the meaning of laugh. For early humankind, laughter was no doubt a temporary respite from a harsh existence. Any time someone made it into the cave before the saber-toothed tiger got him, that was cause for a good laugh. And every time a fellow clan member stubbed his toe on a rock or backed a little too close to the fire, the circuitry was created for appreciating the Three Stooges millions of years later. But it wasn't until the birth of Fu Ling (538-464 B.C.), during the Tai Ming Dynasty in ancient China, that anyone actually took laughter seriously.

Not only was Fu Ling the first comedian in recorded history, but he was the first to describe the Laugh Cycle and the human jestive system. He has been referred to as the "Father of Comedy" (necessity being the mother) and his model of the Laugh Cycle is still used today. According to Fu Ling, the Universe began when God started a joke and will end when the Creator has the Last Laugh. In between, the laughter builds into an ever-increasing crescendo until the final punch-line comes, and we all laugh together.

Fu Ling maintained that the material world provides us with material, and Spirit provides us with joy. The healthy heart heartily laughing uses the joy to digest material, breaking it down into laughter and what Fu Ling called "duty." Laughter is given back to the heavens to create more joy, and duty goes back to the Earth to create more material.

Duty, said Fu Ling, is what we do. The heavier the laughter, the lighter our duty, and the lighter the duty, the better the material. The better the material, the heartier the laughter, and the heartier the laughter, the greater the joy.

Not surprisingly, FUNdamentalists have always taken a special interest in the human jestive system. An early FUNdamentalist, a Russian monk by the name of Yuri Diculus (1440?-1500?) began to wonder if the laughter that we took so much for granted was a reflection of a Farce greater than ourselves. As an experiment, he decided to make a fool of himself. He took to wandering the villages in the middle of winter wearing nothing but a painted-on smile. There, he would invite villagers to tickle him until he lost consciousness. It was during one of those tickle-torture sessions that the monk was struck by enlightening, and became the first to describe the clown chakra as a bright red glow hovering about six inches in front of people's noses. Laughter, he observed, caused the glow to become bigger and brighter. Frowning and undue seriousness–which today we call "irregularhilarity"–caused the clown chakra to shrivel and fade, letting in very little light. Yuri Diculus devoted the rest of his life to traveling the countryside playing and offering jokes, never leaving a village until everyone's clown chakra was brightly glowing.

Discovery of the Human Jestive System

It would be several more centuries before the noted French humorologist, Ray-Pierre Witt (1808-1891) would describe the inner workings of the human jestive system. Witt, best known for discovering and observing humorrhoids, wondered what caused jestive blockages. He spent nearly ten years studying frogs, before concluding that they had no sense of humor. So he turned his keen powers of observation to human subjects. One of the first things he noticed was the strong correlation between laughter and fun. The more people enjoyed life, he observed, the more they laughed. And the more they laughed, the more they enjoyed life.

He also noticed that some people were simply not amused. They could sit through the most hilarious Punch and Judy puppet show or bawdy burlesque performance unmoved, faces clenched in a sour frown. He named this condition "humorrhoids," and set about to discover the cause. Most humorrhoid sufferers, he found, felt a tremendous sense of obligation–and resentment. Witt concluded that lack of laughter had left them duty-bound, resulting in an abnormally enlarged onus. He sent them home with the instructions to let go of some of their duty and spend part of each day playing with little children. When patients returned to him weeks later, he reported, most were smiling for the first time, and their onus had shrunk to nearly normal size.

A student of Ray-Pierre Witt's, the German humorologist Dr. Gustav Wind (1852-1947) added to our understanding of human jestion with his discovery of the importance of irony intake to the skeptic system. In his now-classic book, *How to Live to Be 150 And Never Look a Day Over 100*, Dr. Wind writes of encountering a puzzling phenomenon. A number of people he observed weren't particularly unhappy, and yet had virtually no sense of humor. He enlisted the great German comic, von Leiner, to toss jokes at a group of selected subjects, and not one of them got the joke. Further examination showed these individuals to be "gullible and somewhat dim-witted." (Note: I have quoted here Dr. Wind's exact words. No psychologist nowadays would dare to use the term "dim-witted." It has been replaced by the more politically-correct "clue-deficient.")

Dr. Wind concluded that these subjects were suffering from irony deficiency–an inability to utilize irony to process complex ideas. As a result, these individuals had a tendency to swallow beliefs whole, completely bypassing the skeptic system. By getting these individuals to chew on irony tablets daily, he was able to see an improved response in the skeptic system. And today, some seventy-five years later, pumping ironies is still recommended for jestive health.

How the Jestive System Works

To understand the marvelous process of jestion, let us now follow the laugh cycle through the jestive process. We will begin with some material. As we have already seen, if the material world gives us one thing, it is material. Let us say you are closing your car door, and as you are watching it close, you see your only set of keys still in the ignition. The door closes, and the car automatically locks. Let us also assume you are on your way to someplace Very Important.

Your first impulse may be to do what is called Tantrum Yoga. This is understandable, and in certain circumstances, can be quite helpful. For example, adepts at Tantrum Yoga are able to use their anger to heat their homes in the wintertime. But the primary practice of Tantrum Yoga–holding your breath until God gives you what you want–has been found to be largely ineffective. And while the accompanying stomping, shouting, and hair-pulling does put you in touch with ire consciousness, it tends to block the jestive process.

Jestive health is measured by how quickly one gets to laughter. A Fu Ling master with a fully opened clown chakra, for example, will be rolling on the floor with laughter even before the car door has closed. The average person might have to stimulate the jestive juices by looking in the side mirror and going, "Ha-ha-ha, ha-ha-ha, ha-ha-ha," until the jestive process kicks in. Many practicing FUNdamentalists carry jestive aids, like those Groucho nose-mustache-glasses devices, for just such emergencies.

At the moment when whole-hearted laughter finally

occurs–humorologists call this "ejoculation"–there is a very definite metaphysical reaction where the material is broken down into bubbles of laughter. The heavier the laughter, the more the onus relaxes, allowing us to let go of heavy duty and do whatever light duty is required. In our hypothetical example, this might mean peacefully calling the locksmith (or the lox-smith, if you wanted to have a smoked fish snack while you waited), and making alternative plans to keep your appointment. Your enlightened attitude also improves the quality of material that others get to process. And as Fu Ling observed, this raises the quality of laugh on the planet.

But the jestive process doesn't end there. If your skeptic system is functioning properly, you will immediately be able to utilize any irony that comes your way. In this case, the irony might be the security system that works so well that not even you, the car owner, can get into your car. Chewing on this irony can cause further ejoculation, and it can nourish others by providing an experience they can enjoy vicariously. This can cause a measurable increase in laugh expectancy.

Although there are some in our society who find it crude and vulgar, studies show that ejoculating improves the breathing and lowers the blood pressure because it causes blood vessels to dilate. And anyone would agree this is better than having them die early. Despite what your parents may have told you, we humans have the capacity for prolonged pleasure, and were meant to ejoculate every day!

Some Common Jestive Disorders

Jestive blockages keep us from fun, peace, happiness, and a loving heart. Because they cut off our pipeline to the infinite well of joy, they compromise our wellness and keep us from living as FUNdamentalists. And these jestive disturbances are so unnecessary! It is sad indeed that so many of us suffer needlessly from chronic irregularhilarity and painful humorrhoids when relief and release are so easy and inexpensive. So let's look at some common jestive disorders which block complete jestion and may ultimately compromise our laugh expectancy.

These are, from mildest to most serious:

1. Irregularhilarity
2. Irony Deficiency
3. Humorrhoids
4. Truth Decay

Irregularhilarity

Irregularhilarity is the most common and–if caught early enough–the most treatable jestive disorder. Just about all of us suffer from irregularhilarity from time to time. Irregularhilarity comes from forgetting to laugh, and consequently holding on to material which would be better released. Untreated, irregularhilarity can become chronic and lead to a full-blown case of humorrhoids. Irregularhilarity is most commonly triggered by the overload of information and obligation in our dysFUNsional society–what psychologists now call Contemporary Insanity. A common complaint is Sinatra's Syndrome, a Do-be-do-be-do imbalance caused by a Be deficiency. When faced with the overwhelming demands of life, Sinatra Syndrome sufferers plunge into doing more–they do, do, do until their entire existence is doo-doo. And the overload of information may cause the skeptic system to back up, choking off the jocular vein.

Fortunately, this disorder is easily treatable. For one thing, laughsitives can be bought over-the-counter at any book or tape store (humor section), as well as toy stores, and clown supply houses. More controversial are the uses of chemical or even herbal laughsitives, such as sillium. Because the enlarged onus tends to block the laugh force, the best treatment involves priming the pump by inducing laughter. Simply repeating the mantra "Ha-ha-ha" in rapid succession will usually cause the laugh cycle to kick in on its own accord. In a few extreme cases, some simple lifestyle changes might be in order, like quitting your job and joining the circus.

Irony Deficiency

Here is something ironic: We live at a time when our diets are richer in irony than ever before in human history, yet millions of us suffer from that silent crippler, irony deficiency. How is that possible? Well, I will tell you. What we call "irony deficiency" is not so much a deficiency in irony itself, but an inability to utilize the abundance of irony all around us. The jestive system uses irony to help us ruminate on ideas and break them down before we swallow them. When we have difficulty in our irony uptake, these ironies pass through us without being digested. This can lead to clue-deficiency, assaholism and ultimately, truth decay. Ironically, even professional comedians who pump ironies for a living may still be unable to process ironies in their own lives.

Release Jestive Blockages

Irony deficiency has been called a social disease because it is often transmitted through the mass media. For example, it is now known that sleazium, a key element found in daytime television, interferes with our ability to utilize irony. Not only that, but the constant barrage of information most of us get through television, radio, junk mail, junk faxes, email, etc., allow many ironies to pass through our systems undetected and unused. Irony deficiency is quite common among infomaniacs–people so addicted to information that they can't go more than an hour without getting some. Your typical raving infomaniac will notice no irony in spending all of his waking hours finding out about life instead of actually living it.

Do you suffer from irony deficiency? Take this simple test:

- Do you spend most of your waking hours at a job wishing for the time to pass quickly?
- Would you rather drive around aimlessly for forty-five minutes than "waste time" asking for directions?
- Do you say your cat has been "fixed" even though he wasn't broken until you "fixed" him?

If you answered "yes" to any of the above questions, you need to up your intake of irony.

Humorrhoids

Humorrhoids are a chronic condition, characterized by undue seriousness, and particularly the inability to laugh at oneself. If untreated, this condition can lead to complete atrophy of the jocular vein. In its intermediate stages, humorrhoids can cause difficulty ejoculating. Advanced-stage humorrhoid sufferers may lose their ability to ejoculate entirely, and may be unable to pass anything except heavy judgments.

Many humorologists believe that humorrhoids are caused by having a malnourished inner child. Humorrhoid patients often report growing up in a dysFUNsional household, and have abnormally low levels of sillium. Sillium is a natural substance, found in healthy families, which causes giggles in children and adults alike. Medical studies show that sillium levels rise dramatically during play, and humorrhoids can often be treated with high doses of Duck Soup.

Are you suffering from humorrhoids? Watch for these danger signals:

1. You find yourself saying, "This is definitely not funny," or worse yet, "I fail to see the humor here."
2. You recently broke a mirror-by looking into it.
3. Old friends you meet on the street ask if you've recently died.
4. You start getting invited to Assaholics Anonymous meetings.

Truth Decay

When irony deficiency and humorrhoids go untreated for any period of time and toxic ideas are allowed to worm their way in between the thoughts, the result is truth decay, the most laugh-threatening of all jestive disorders. After years of being unable to use irony to break down toxic beliefs, the skeptic system begins to overflow with B.S. and slowly chokes off the jocular, stopping the flow of joy to the heart. The first symptom of truth decay might very well be smartyrdom–the willingness to sacrifice being happy for being right. From smartyrdom, it is an all-too-easy step to full-blown assaholism.

Fortunately, my own smartyrdom was cured early on in my apprenticeship with Harry Cohen Baba. One day he said to me, "You're pretty smart, right?"

I told him I thought I was pretty smart.

"Are you happy?" he asked.

"Not particularly," I said.

"You're not happy?" he answered rhetorically. "What's so smart about that? If you had any smarts, you'd use them to get happy!" With these words, my trance was transformed and I stopped being a smartyr.

As truth decay advances, the swelling of the onus may become so painful that the sufferer becomes addicted to complaining. These "whinos" may also become dope addicts, who keep attracting the same dopes–usually assaholics–into their lives again and again. Studies show that whinos and assaholics will often marry one another. The result is the dysFUNsional family.

Without the nourishment that comes from laughter, joy, and play, truth decay victims are in danger of losing every truth in their head. They commonly suffer from what is commonly called "malconclusion"–where each truth comes in malformed or crooked. The tragic final stage of truth decay is kind of a "spiritual Alzheimer's" –where you forget there is any fun in life whatsoever. As bad as it is, truth decay is treatable at any stage. For immediate and dramatic results, four out of five transcendentists recommend mental flossing daily to remove toxic feelings and beliefs that get stuck between thoughts.

The Underlying Causes of Jestive Problems

Underlying truth decay, and all of the other jestive malfunctions are the attitudes and practices of our dysFUNsional society. These include:

1. Oughtism
2. Racism
3. Contemporary Insanity

When I first met Harry Cohen Baba, I suffered from oughtism. I'd been taking oughtas all my life. Many times, I had been advised to go to a co-dependency group. I would have, too, if only I could have found someone to go with. Being oughtistic, I was prepared to let my new teacher oughta me around. But he wouldn't. Each morning I would ask him what I should do, and each morning he would answer with a shrug. Because I was so trained to follow oughtas, my oughtanomic nervous system shut down completely. I was at wit's end, and if you're a Fu Ling practitioner, that is not a good place to be. But once again, the Garment Center Saint came to the rescue. "You're wasting your time worrying about what other people think," he told me. "You know why? Because most people don't think."

I am embarrassed to admit this, but I grew up in a racist family. My parents imbued me with the idea that life is a race, and whoever gets there first wins. Unfortunately, they never bothered to tell me where exactly we were racing to. And so I started my life running fool-speed-ahead in all directions simultaneously. Harry Cohen Baba soon put an end to my racist behavior. After watching me run hither and yon for several days, he asked me, "Where are you right now?"

"What do you mean?" I asked.

"I mean," he said, "physically right now, where are you?"

"I'm right here," I answered.

"Good," he said. "Now imagine it's later and you go somewhere else. Where are you then?"

"Well, I suppose I'll be there."

"Okay, now suppose I am there with you and ask you where you are. What are you gonna tell me?"

"I guess I'll say 'I'm here.'"

"So if you're still going to be here after all that coming and going, what's the rush?"

At that moment I realized that no matter where I went I could never escape being "here." And if there was a there to get to, that was neither here nor there, because even when I got there I would still be here. That's when I decided to stop racing. Since that time I simply pretend that I am a couple of laps ahead and everyone else is trying to catch up with me. This has worked better than you can imagine.

Both oughtism and racism have contributed to a condition I call Contemporary Insanity–the belief that we have to be doing and making in order to be worthy. This is particularly true of men, who think that by building, building, building, they will overcome their fear of not being enough, and what they construct will become their living monument. In psychological circles, this is known as an unresolved edifice complex. This worship of the man-made leaves millions of pilgrims stuck on the highway of life each morning as they go to jobs they don't really like to buy things they don't really need to impress people they don't really know. And because so many of these unfortunate souls are irony-deficient, this huge irony passes through their skeptic systems largely undigested.

The result of all this contemporary insanity is stress, and I cannot stress enough how stressful stress is. In fact, all of this rushing around to get nowhere has given us a big fat case of emotion sickness. No wonder we are beginning to see recovery groups like Overachievers Anonymous (they have a 24-step program). Fortunately, the human jestive system is remarkably resilient, and with the investment of just a few hours a week, your jestive health can be restored.

Swami's Recipe for Duck Soup

Seven Ways to Prevent Truth Decay:

1. Use Mental Floss Daily
2. Start Each Day with a Good Laughsitive
3. Just Say No
4. Do a Slow
5. Whatever It Is, Peace on It!
6. Practice the Science of I-Don't-Mind
7. Don't Forget Pumping Ironies!

Use Mental Floss Daily

When people come to me suffering from hindered-jestion, the first thing I do is check their flossing habits. It's dollars to doughnuts they've never used mental floss. Why is it that the easiest things are the ones we most often neglect? How difficult can it be to take a few moments every day, hold your thumb and forefinger on either side of your ears, and move them back and forth gently? Whenever stress, confusion, or irregularhilarity is starting to get the best of you, I recommend that you stop and floss. Stuck in traffic? Take those hands off the steering wheel (no need to hold the wheel when the car isn't moving) and floss. Trapped in a social setting with an assaholic or whino? There's no law that says you can't whip the floss out on the spot and clear your thoughts.

But don't take my word for it. The American Transcendental Association tells us that mental floss is the easiest way to prevent truth loss. That gentle back-and-forth motion dislodges the gunk that can get stuck in our heads over the course of an average day, not to mention the excess flossophy that has accumulated from years of schooling. And mental floss is completely safe for children! In fact, I recommend that your entire family floss together at least once a day. Remember, the laugh you save may be your own!

Start Each Day with a Good Laughsitive

Even if you don't suffer from irregularhilarity, a natural laughsitive will freshen the mind after a good flossing. Some folks prefer those telephone or Internet joke lines to start the day off right. Others enjoy listening to canned laughter until their own jestive juices begin flowing. Still others get a chuckle watching or listening to their children. Yes, laughsitives are everywhere abundant, and as soon as you begin noticing them, you will find yourself injesting laughsitives often during the day.

Some people with persistent irregularhilarity or chronic humorrhoids find they need to use herbal or even chemical laughsitives. A few words of caution here: First of all, prolonged use of laughsitives can result in comical dependency. Secondly, while certain herbal laughsitives are high in sillium, possession of such for the purpose of having fun is still illegal. Medical uses, however, continue to proliferate, and I have it on good authority that Willie Nelson is set to release a new musical tribute to the substance, "You Were Prozac 'Fore Prozac Turned Pro."

But I would be remiss if I didn't tell you that there is a two-letter word that is more effective than any drug when it comes to shrinking the onus and restoring regularhilarity. That word is "no."

Just Say No

I've never been able to understand why "just say no" has become associated with drugs. Believe me, if we just said no when we meant no, we wouldn't need drugs. Nothing shrinks a swollen onus like the magical one-word mantra, "No." Come on now, say it with me please. No. No. No. NO-NO-NO-NO-NO! Doesn't that feel good? Each time you utter that magic word, obligation dissolves and you release a little bit of the duty that is constipating your life.

I want you to think back to when you were two years old and just learning about the pleasure of saying no. You were a regular no-it-all, weren't you? And then what happened? Your parents told you to just say no to saying no, and all of a sudden you didn't no anything anymore. And if you can't say no, then you can't really say yes. So you say yes when you mean no, and you end up resenting it. This is how people become whinos.

I speak from experience because when I came to Harry Cohen Baba, I was oughtistic. The Garment Center Saint had me limit my vocabulary to a single word for an entire month. And that word was "No." This was particularly difficult when my parents or other loved ones called. But Harry Cohen Baba was adamant: "To no 'em is to love 'em." He insisted that saying no fostered unconditional love, because if people still loved you after you denied them everything, their love must be unconditional. Saying no was very difficult for me, but I persisted. You can't imagine what a sense of pride and accomplishment I felt when Harry Cohen Baba told me, "You are getting no-aware fast. This is good. Now you will stand for something instead of standing for anything anyone thinks you'll stand for. So just keep following your No's."

Do a Slow

While many authorities recommend fasting as an antidote to Contemporary Insanity, I disagree. I think things are already too fast, so I recommend slowing. If you are already experiencing some early signs of truth decay, I would do a one-day slow immediately! On the day of your slow, take as long to open your eyes as it takes the sun to come over the horizon. When you get out of bed, be sure to get out of bed one cell at a time. And when you walk into the kitchen for your one meal of the day–believe me, that is all you will have time for–pretend you are following in an ant's footsteps, and don't miss any! Chew each bite of food until you can't remember if you had any food in your mouth in the first place.

When you are done eating, you may still have some time left over. I suggest you use this time to brush up on your Languish Arts skills. You might begin with some 'robics. That is where you sit in your robe and listen to the latest Marcel Marceau CD–it's called The Sounds of Silence. (If you are into "easy listening," believe me, it doesn't get any easier than this.) Do some bench presses, using your *gluteus maximus* to press against the bench. Oh, and be sure to watch lots of baseball. Now I must tell you that prolonged slowing can lead to an altered state of consciousness. I once did a 40-day slow, and after that I couldn't watch baseball anymore. It simply moved too quickly for me to follow. But I will tell you, during my 40-day slow, I accomplished a life-long dream. I have always wanted to live to be 100, and thanks to slowing I've been able to achieve that goal in half the time!

Whatever It Is, Peace on It!

People often comment on how peaceful I seem. These are generally people who don't know me. So I tell them the key to peace is developing peace within. If everyone just felt a little peace, we'd have a little peace here and a little peace there, and this would eventually add up to one big peace everywhere. And the key to peace is allowing only peaceful words to pass your lips, no matter what you are feeling. So next time you feel yourself about to get really upset, speak your peace. Utter the peace mantra, "Ah, peace on it!" You've got a busy day ahead and your karma won't start? "Peace on it!" The IRS has chosen you–and it isn't because you're the ten millionth tax payer and they want to give you a prize. Peace on it. Yes, whatever happens, shout "Peace on it!"

This is better than saying "Dammit!" Here's why: Usually, you want to shout "dammit!" when things aren't flowing. But if the damn flow isn't flowing, it must already be dammed, right? Only a damn fool would want to damn it more. So when things seem stuck, shout "Undamn it!" This makes more sense. If things seem cursed already, who needs more cursing? Why not shout "blesses" instead?

And forget about saying things like "darn it." I just finished a fascinating book called *Planet of the Darned* by the noted Greek futurist, Xavier Onassis. He maintains that using the word "darn" evokes in your life persistent irritating phenomena, which he calls "darnation." While darnation is a far milder form of suffering than damnation, it can still make your life a living heck. According to Onassis, each time you say something like, "Well, I'll be darned," you bring into your life the gol-durnedest things–flat tires, answering machines that eat messages, paper cuts, bitten tongues, bad coffee, nauseating perfume in the seat next to you on a five-hour flight–and all kinds of other dadblasted, dadburned shucks.

So that's why I say stick with "Peace on it!"

Practice the Science of I-Don't-Mind

Science of Mind is great for planting seeds, but for jestive health nothing beats the Science of I-Don't-Mind. I am a big believer in the power of Mind. In fact, I used to "treat" for everything. Whatever I wanted in my life, I did a prayer treatment for it. One day, Harry Cohen Baba asked me what I was doing. I told him I was "treating." He motioned toward the sky and said, "He's the Big Spender. Let Him treat."

And it's been God's treat ever since.

Now I realize how hard it is to let go of outcome–especially if the outcome is income. And it's true that if you want to achieve anything in life, you must have intention. But beware of becoming too intense. A little intention is good for you, but if you're under too much intention you could snap. If you find yourself suffering from chronic intention, you might try practicing the Science of I-Don't-Mind. I've spoken to a lot of recovering assaholics who have found their peace that way.

One more thing: Don't get attached to letting go. Before you can really let go, you have to let go of letting go. And beware of pretending you have let go when you haven't. I'll never forget the time Harry Cohen Baba walked into my room during a time of great stress and asked how everything was going.

"Everything is perfect," was my reply.

"I'm glad to hear you say that," he said, "because I just stepped in some dog perfection and I think I just tracked it across your new meditation rug." This was indeed a perfect opportunity for me to let go, which I did in an hour-long Tantrum Yoga session.

Don't Forget Pumping Ironies!

Irony deficiency is a funny disease. Seeing a doctor won't help–but seeing a paradox will. To help you begin your daily regimen of pumping ironies, I offer a few irony tablets for you to chew on:

- A commercial for Velveeta tells us, "Accept no substitutes." This means someone is making imitation Velveeta.
- The movie producer Sam Goldwyn once told employees, "I don't want any yes-men around me. I want people to tell me the truth even if it costs them their jobs."
- Psychic fair canceled-due to unforeseen circumstances.
- And if you want to chew on a particularly bitter irony, try this one: Holy War.

Another Zen Cohen

Harry Cohen Baba was once asked how one could remain happy despite the stresses of life, and he told the following parable: Two psychiatrists each had their practice in the same building for twenty-five years, but had never spoken. After a quarter-century in practice, one of them still appeared young and upbeat. The other looked old and beat up. One day, they found themselves on the elevator together. Unable to contain his curiosity, the prematurely-aged psychiatrist began a conversation with his colleague. "I've got to know," he began. "How can you spend twenty-five years listening to people's problems and still look so bright and cheerful?"

"Who listens?" was the reply.

Any More Questions?

Dear Swami:
You know how there's this metabolic "set-point" which governs our body weight–and slows our weight loss when we're dieting? Well, now I hear that each of us has an "emotional set-point" which determines our level of happiness. According to this theory, no matter how good things get, we're genetically programmed to be at a certain level of happiness, and no happier. As someone who has always been somewhat

> grouchy and uptight, I have been motivated to take personal growth workshops in hopes of getting an attitude adjustment. But if this theory is true, then I'm wasting my time. Help me out, Swami. Is there any hope for tinkering with my happiness set-point? Or am I doomed to spend the rest of my days grumpy and tense?
>
> *Doug Garnett*
> *Towson, Maryland*

Dear Doug:

Well, I have some bad news and some good news. The bad news is, there is indeed an emotional set-point that determines one's level of happiness. And there's more bad news: cognitive therapy and personal growth workshops will not appreciably change this set-point. However, there is a glimmer of hope. Apparently this emotional set-point can be altered surgically. There is an experimental procedure where they go in through your navel, loosen it a couple of turns–and you become less of a tight-ass.

> Dear Swami:
>
> Lately, I've been waking up feeling listless. This is particularly frustrating because I have so much to do. The doctors can find no physical problem, yet I can't seem to muster the energy to do all those things I should. How can I get rid of this listlessness?
>
> *Kay Ottick*
> *Burbank, California*

Dear Kay:

Actually, you should be cultivating listlessness. Sounds like you have too many lists in your life already, and that is what is exhausting you. I suggest giving yourself two days a week to totally ignore all of your lists. You should have only one item on your To Do list on those days: BE LISTLESS!

Don't plan a thing. You'll be delighted at how enjoyable that listless feeling can be. Remember, a little listing is normal as you sail through life–but list too much and you'll capsize.

Dear Swami:
Can two negatives ever make a positive?

Atwood B. Goode
Kennett Square, Pennsylvania

Dear Atwood:

Sure, and I just heard a heartwarming story that proves it. I recently met a man who suffers from both dyslexia and paranoia. But it has worked out splendidly. He is convinced the Universe is conspiring to make him happy.

Dear Swami:
I read somewhere that extremely low frequencies can cause depression. Is that true?

Lola Beado
Newton, Massachusetts

Dear Lola:

Yes, there is some truth to that. Several years ago, a study showed that people whose frequency was once or twice a year tended to be more depressed than those whose frequency was let's say, three times a week. But thanks to our remarkable capacity for optimism and resiliency, this need not always be true. I remember years ago meeting a man whose frequency was extremely low. And yet, I've never seen anyone happier or more aglow. I had to ask how he did it. I said, "You've just told me your frequency is once every six years, and yet you're smiling as if you're the happiest man on earth. Why is that?"

"Because tonight's the night," he replied.

Swami's Omwork Assignment:

Make Instant Duck Soup for Immediate Jestive Relief

Do you ever wake up in the morning, look in the mirror, and think to yourself, "I cannot interface with that outerface?" This is the first sign of irregularhilarity. The next time you find yourself not having fun–and not having fun not having fun–here's a sound exercise guaranteed to provide jestive relief and revitalize your laugh force:

To activate all five laugh centers of the body, it is necessary to experience the fool range of laughter, from guffaws on up to titters. Yes, laughter is an in-body experience so we need to get those bubbles of laughter to every part of the body.

Let's begin with a good guffaw–HOO HOO HOO HOO–coming from the base of the body. This helps you laugh at your own base instincts.

Now on up to the solar plexus with a good belly laugh, HO HO HO. Did you know that laughing at your own belly reduces shame and makes food taste better?

Then make the vowel sound "ah" with a HA HA HA–good hearty laughter coming right from the heart.

Then up to the throat and chuckle, HEH HEH HEH. That's right. Bring out your inner Beavis and Butthead.

And on up to the third eye, and titter HEE HEE HEE. Believe me, you are tittering on the edge of enlightenment.

And now, reverse those vowel sounds, moving downward through all five laugh centers.

Yes, there's nothing like a good vowel movement to clear the pipes and extend your laugh span. But, you ask, what if there's nothing funny? It doesn't matter. Just because it isn't funny doesn't mean you can't laugh. In fact, laughter helps the most when things aren't funny.

Part III

Drive your Karma, Curb your Dogma

Life is a Mannafestival

Life is a mannafestival, the FUNdamentalist scriptures tell us, and it is our mannafest destiny to manifest manna–and to have fun doing it. Rich or poor, it doesn't matter. All of us are to the manna born. Well, I have to admit that during my early days with Harry Cohen Baba, I had my doubts about this. I had spent the entire previous year going through what I call my Baroque period–you know, so Baroque I was Haydn from the landlord. One Wednesday at the weekly Pinochle game, I challenged the idea of life being one big manna fest. "What about the suffering of those who have nothing to eat?" I protested.

"Hey, I'll do you one better," the Garment Center Saint replied as he melded his customary flush in hearts. "What about the suffering of those who have plenty to eat?"

"If life is such a manna fest," I persisted, "how come I'm not manifesting manna? Is it my karma?" I knew that Harry Cohen Baba had been working on karmas for years, and had even rebuilt a few in his day.

"Could be," he replied. "Why don't you bring your karma in tomorrow morning and we'll have a look under the hood."

So the next morning I dutifully brought my karma in for inspection. After poking and probing and pacing and saying, "Mmmh," and "Hunhh," several times, he asked me pointedly, "Do you know how your karma works?"

I was a little embarrassed to admit it, but even though I'd been using it to get around my entire lifetime, I knew nothing about the inner workings (or, for that matter, the outer workings) of my karma. "No," I said quietly, "I've never really thought about what actually makes a karma go, but doesn't it have something to do with internal combustion?"

"Well, yes," he replied, "the karmas we have grown up with seem to get driven by lots of friction and internal combustion. But this can be quite stressful, not to mention the wear and tear on the parts. In this new millennium, you can expect to see a lot more clean-burning karmas running on esteem."

"So esteem is karma fuel?" I asked.

"Not exactly," he replied. "Any material in life we laugh at is fuel for our karma. When we add a spark of joy to any painful material in our lives, this causes an explosion of mirth–and this bubbling of laughter through the jestive system causes esteem to rise. This rising esteem, in turn, empowers our karma–and we are on our way to the mannafestival."

"Well," I said, "I have had trouble starting my karma lately. Could it be I'm out of fuel?"

"Not a chance!" Harry Cohen Baba chuckled. "Believe me, you have enough material in there to go on fueling yourself for a long, long time. Your main problem is with your intake manna fold."

"My what?"

"Your intake manna fold is all gunked up with sludge. If your intake manna fold isn't letting enough joy in, even if you try to jumpstart your karma by going 'ha ha ha ha ha,' it won't catch."

I nodded and he continued. "See this here? Your karma is all dented. Like most of us, you've been rear-ended a few times, right? And here, see? Your front end has been crunched too. This is a sure indication of bad breaks."

"Yes," I agreed, "I've definitely had some bad breaks recently."

"Don't worry," he reassured me. When we get done with you, your Master Cylinder will be so filled with manna, you will never be troubled by bad breaks again."

He proceeded to poke around a little more. Suddenly, he

cried out, "Aha! I think I found it! You've got a trance-mission problem!"

"Transmission?" I asked.

"Yes," he said with a triumphant smile. "You're not fully engaged so you can't quite get your karma in gear. No wonder you've lost so much of your drive. My guess is you've been in a trance and forgotten your mission. You'll never make it to the mannafestival that way."

"What are you driving at?" I asked. "I thought manna is something we're given automatically. You know–manna falling from the skies?"

"Bird poop falls from the skies," said the Garment Center Saint with a chuckle. "Manna you gotta manifest. You see, God doesn't generally drop food from the heavens. That was a misinterpretation of a coincidental event. It so happened that the Hebrews were starving in the desert just as God was cleaning out His pantry. You know that stuff about how matter can neither be created nor destroyed? The fact is, God is a saver. He very rarely throws anything away. But how long can you save the crumbs from the bottom of the chip bag? He figured, what the heck, it's my Universe, I can dump. So He dumped. The Jews just happened to come by at the right time."

"That's amazing. I did not know that," I said in true awe. Not only was my beloved teacher a crack karma mechanic, but he was a theologian too.

"Look," Harry Cohen Baba continued, "God loves us and wants the best for us. But He certainly doesn't want us helplessly stuck in the feed-us position, begging for peanuts like some squirrel. So He gave us the wherewithal to mannafacture our own manna–you know it as Duck Soup. When we express ourselves joyfully in the world, we are nourishing not just ourselves but others as well."

"But what about my karma?" I wanted to know.

"Your karma is the vehicle you have chosen to bring your own batch of Duck Soup to the mannafestival. And your expressway is whichever route you take to get there–any way you enjoy expressing yourself will work. The problem with most people is, they never even get their karma out of the garage. They never find their expressway. And they never make it to the mannafestival. So if you want to manifest manna, the first thing you gotta do is drive your own karma."

Driving Your Own Karma

In the old days, people actually used to believe that we were driven by our karma. But now we are coming to realize that we do indeed drive our own karma. No longer can we listen to political or spiritual leaders who say, "Leave the driving to us." After all, if we were meant to have group karma, it would be called "busma," would it not?

I must admit, this notion of driving my karma was a little confusing at first. So I busied myself doing meticulous karma care, thinking that if my karma were clean enough I would manifest manna. But after several weeks of purification and meditation, my spiritual pantry was as bare as the day I first arrived at Harry Cohen Baba's doorstep.

Seeing my frustration, the Garment Centered One offered some advice. "Look *boychick*," he began, "you can't spend all your time at the self-help karma wash. Meditation is fine, but you have to stop polishing your karma long enough to take it out for a spin. You know, see what that baby can do. Your karma is useless unless you take it somewhere."

"But where should I go?" I asked.

"You have to get out on the expressway," he repeated.

"You mean like I-95?" I asked.

"I-whatever," he answered impatiently, "as long as it begins with 'I.' Each of us must find our own expressway. That's why we see so many clogged arteries nowadays. Because too many of us are stuck on someone else's expressway."

"So how do I find my expressway?" I persisted.

"Finally, you ask the right question!" he laughed. "Any way

you express that turns material into laughter is your expressway. You're in the driver's seat, pal. All you need to do to get that manna flowing through the intake manna fold is to get your karma moving. You'll get to the mannafestival in no time. Just stay on that expressway."

"But what about getting off?" I asked.

"Believe me," he said, "if you're on the right expressway, getting off will be no problem. I guarantee it, you will get off a heckuva lot more than you're getting off right now."

What Kind of Karma Should I Drive?

Everybody has a karma to drive, everybody on the physical plane anyway. And it doesn't really matter what kind of karma you drive as long as it puts you on the expressway. Chances are, before you incarnated, you went to a karma dealer, or even a used karma lot. There, you chose a vehicle that fit your style. So I suggest you take a look at the karma you are already driving (yes, trade-ins are possible–I will say more about that later) and consider the following questions: Is your karma a big karma, or a little karma? A gas-guzzler or one of those fuel-efficient high-economy karmas? A sporty model or a cheap pick-up? An elegant Continental or a beat-up bug? Maybe your karma is an old Dodge. Or one of those flashy convertibles. You know the type. Every time the weather changes, they convert.

You might notice you're driving the same karma your father drove. Or, you might say, "Are you kidding? I wouldn't be caught dead with a karma like that!" And so you've gone and got yourself a sleek racing karma. But the thing to remember is, there is no race. The bottom line is, life is a joyride–and any karma that gets you on the expressway will do.

What If My Karma Won't Shift?

Eventually, when driving your own karma you will sense it is time to move into a higher gear. But what if your karma refuses to shift? If your first impulse is to depress the clutch, you are forgetting that you are driving an automatic. There is no need for clutching, and certainly no need for depression. Just relax and remember the mantra, "Shift happens." This is easy to say of course until the shift actually hits the fanbelt. Then you will probably ask yourself, "Why is this shift happening to me?"

Don't worry. As was my case, you are probably suffering from a simple trance-mission problem. Ask yourself if you are in a trance that keeps you in low-gear, and remember your mission. Relax the clutch, let laughter lubricate your gearbox, and you will find your karma shifting effortlessly.

How Do I Know when It's Time to Get a New Karma?

How many times have you muttered to yourself, "My karma just ain't running right?" If you find yourself complaining that your old karma is a lemon, it may be time to fix it, trade it in, or get a brand new one. As Harry Cohen Baba used to say, "If you're tired of the same old Saab story, it's time to try an Evolvo."

And driving your karma is a two-way street. If you faithfully service your karma, your karma will faithfully service you. First of all, I recommend a periodic karma wash, and not just because I'm in the business. I hate to be the one to tell you this, but you may be suffering from psychic b.o.–we call it bodhi odor–that happens to any karma with high mileage. And let's be honest. We smelled in past lives. Some of us really stunk, and that stink is going to stick. So the first thing I would recommend is bringing that dirty karma in for a hose-down, especially the underside. The underside of your karma picks up some pretty foul stuff over the course of lifetimes.

And thanks to new liberal lending policies, you can actually trade in your old karma for a new one. One way is through "pre-incarnation." That is where you make your karma payments early, and you start working on extra credit for your next lifetime. It's not a guarantee, but if you take on this post-graduate work, your Father will probably reward you with a brand new karma. The more common way nowadays to be able to afford a new karma before your old one is completely paid off is by using your Ascended Mastercard ("Don't leave Om without it"). The Ascended Mastercard is kind of a karmic debit card. Not only can you borrow against future good deeds, but you get a one-time "Get Out of Hell Free" card. Personally, I prefer leasing. You lease your karma, and then every year you re-lease it until one year you release it.

Watch Out for Those Dogmas!

It's a common tale. You are blithely driving your karma down the expressway and wham! You run smack into somebody's pet dogma. And you are late for the mannafestival–or you might never get there. That's why Harry Cohen Baba was adamant about his second rule for manifesting manna. Not only do you have to drive your karma, but you have to curb your dogma as well.

Now it's true that we human beings have had dogmas since the dawn of recorded history. This is understandable. You cannot imagine how comforting it is to curl up with a warm, fuzzy dogma on a dark night of the soul. Or to take him out to the park and watch him chase other dogmas and bark at strangers. Some dogma-lovers keep them around for protection. It's reassuring to have a guard dogma to scare away frightening thoughts–and it's great to have a loyal companion to fetch you an explanation when you get home from a hard day at the office. And dogmas come in all varieties. Some people like big, dumb dogmas, and others prefer squeaky, little, irritating ones. And, hey, someone needs to stand up for the underdogma. Yes, dogma is truly man's best friend.

Now some of you may be saying, why not let sleeping dogmas lie? But what about dogmas that bark so loudly we cannot hear the laugh track? Or dogmas that run wild and get into everyone's garbage? And worse yet, what about rabid dogmas that bite? I know, I know. You are probably saying, "It isn't my dogma making the mess, it's my neighbor's dogma." And indeed, people do unleash their dogmas irresponsibly. That is why it is so important to teach your dogma to heal. A properly-trained dogma never chases karmas.

It is a fact of life. Dogmas have sharp teeth, and when backed against the wall, they have been known to snap. As a dogma-owner, it is your responsibility to see that your dogma doesn't bite, and if it does...well, sometimes a vicious dogma has to be put down. Another fact of life is that dogmas get sick and old. Perhaps you've spent years taking care of a tired old dogma, and it's time to put that old dogma to sleep.

It is sad when you must give up a loyal dogma like that, so I say, enjoy your dogma while it is alive and playful. My FUNdamentalist dogma, which I have enjoyed for many years, is a great source of laughter and play. And you know how uncanny it is the way dogma owners come to resemble their dogmas. So you can have a dogma–it's fine. But just make sure your dogma doesn't mess on your neighbor's lawn. And know that on Nonjudgment Day, all our dogmas will run free, and I guarantee they won't bother a soul.

Mannapause and How to Get Through It

Although it is our natural state to manifest manna, sometimes the manna just isn't flowing in the manna we've become accustomed to. This is known as mannapause. All of us–men and women–experience mannapause sometime in our lives. I remember when I was going through mannapause. I would get hot flashes of brilliance–and yet there would be little or no flow of prosperity. And nothing was funny. I would start to laugh and then stop in the middle, just like that. As usual, Harry Cohen Baba helped me immensely.

"Oh, you're just going through a mid-laugh crisis," he told me. "This often accompanies mannapause."

"But what do I do?" I asked, more than a little concerned.

"You see?" he said. "That's just the problem. You've been focusing too much on your duty. Personally, I think you've spent too much of your life being a doer. So why not change the pattern and do a beer instead? And while you're sipping a cool one out on the fire escape, think about what has caused the blockage. Is it your karma, or your dogma?"

So I followed the Garment Center Saint's advice and began to let my thoughts flow. Well, it was true. My karma had been running a bit rough lately, and had little of the old pick-up. But then I started thinking about my faithful old dogma, and that's when I saw the problem. Back when I was a child living in a dysFUNsional family, I adopted a stray dogma. This dogma was the belief that if I expected things to turn out poorly, I would never be disappointed. Now I really loved this old dogma. You can't imagine what a comfort it was for me to know that whatever happened in my family, this dogma would make me feel better. But now I realized that the old saying was true. You can't teach an old dogma new tricks. To make it through mannapause, I would have to give up my pet belief. Even so, I was reluctant.

"That dogma protected me," I protested. "What am I going to do about the negative stuff that shows up in my life now?"

"Think of life as photography," the Garment Centered One answered, "and use the negatives to develop."

It took a little while, but I made it through mannapause. The manna started flowing, and it is has never really stopped. And that's how I learned first-hand about mannapause and mid-laugh crisis. So I offer here my guidelines for making it though this trying time–without trying too hard:

1. Look at that Heavy Duty as Fertilizer
2. Get up off Your Assets
3. It's Not Mid-Laugh Crisis–It's "Intermission"
4. Start an Inner Child Care Center
5. If Nothing Works–Do Nothing!

Look at that Heavy Duty as Fertilizer

Quite often, mannapause is accompanied by a feeling of being overwhelmed by heavy duty. It is not uncommon for people to turn creative juices inward and begin obsessing about problems. All this stewing can keep them from mannafesting manna. After all, how can you manifest when all of your energy is spent manifestering? This was my problem. Once I gave away my dogma, I came face to face with all the times I had been hurt. Once again, Harry Cohen Baba came to the rescue.

"I realize that I've been unable to drive my karma lately because I can't stop thinking about all these hurts," I told him.

"Well," he said, "the true Fu Ling master can take any situation and turn it into laughter and play. You have to use all of those hurts to your advantage. The next time you feel hurt, think of that old rent-a-karma commercial–'Let hurts put you in the driver's seat.' I guarantee, you'll be back behind the wheel of your karma and cruising on the expressway in no time."

Then he told me about an ancient Chinese path he had studied. It was the Chinese art of everyday living, and it was called Fung Shun. The Fung Shun masters tell us that the heavy duty we are stepping in is fertilizer. Everyone gets fertilizer. Fertilizer happens. The key question is, now that you have all this fertilizer, what are you going to plant? The Fu Ling master uses this fertilizer to create funny material that nourishes others. And let's face it, the more you make people laugh, the less likely they are to sic their dogma on you.

Get up off Your Assets

If you truly want to get out onto the danceflow, you've got to move your assets. If you don't shake your assets, nobody is going to see them. The problem is, most of us don't know our assets from a hole in the ground. And this is mainly because our economic system equates self-worth with net worth.

See, the free enterprise system, like everything else, has its upside and downside. And for years, we have had things upside down. There's been too much attention paid to the income, and not enough to the outcome. Instead of lustily and passionately pursuing their heart's desire, most folks have been on the sell-a-bit path, selling a bit of themselves each day until they have sold out completely. The good news is, more and more people are listening to their higher self instead of their hired self. And they are wholeheartedly immersing themselves in the "free enter prize system." That is where they realize that we all receive a free gift just for entering–which means each one of us is already a winner. So remember, you are one-of-a-kind-just like everyone else.

It's Not Mid-Laugh Crisis- It's "Intermission"

In his seminal book, From *Peter Pan to Peter Panic*, Dr. Adam Zappel reframes male mid-laugh crisis as "intermission." Intermission, Dr. Zappel writes, is the time when we take a break and examine our mission during the first act of our life and see if it is the mission we want for the second act. Not only men, but women too, are likely to experience "stage fright" as they face the second act of life. "Not to worry," says Dr. Zappel. "Every new stage can be frightening at first."

The solution, he says, is to find a mission in life that gives you that tingle of excitement. In his words, we need to get a "heart-on" for something. "When your heart is engorged with desire to produce something loving and useful," he writes, "you have a heart-on." I think he's absolutely right. Maybe if more of us lived in this state of heightened spiritual arousal, we'd have more people making love to the world and fewer people screwing it.

Start an Inner Child Care Center

People come to me all the time complaining that their jobs aren't fun or they are being discriminated against at work because of their FUNdamentalist faith. My suggestion for those people who want an alternative to their dysFUNsional work environment is, start an Inner Child Care Center. Think of all your fellow sufferers in today's workaholic business world who have to drag their inner children to work with them every day. These poor inner children can suffer severe boredom and spiritual deprivation in these dysFUNsional settings. Personally, I think this borders on inner child abuse. And we all know an abused inner child can wreak havoc at home with unpredictable emotional outbursts, not to mention inbursts.

Here's how the Inner Child Care Center works: Every

morning, your clients drop off their inner children at your home–as inner children are invisible, they take up very little space and are easy to travel with in groups. No institutional kitchens or bathrooms are required, and you can take field trips in a Miata. Most of the program can evolve out of what feels like fun to you, although you can ask your clients for input: And what would your inner child like to do today? Imagine spending your day finger-painting, bike riding, playing video games, going to the zoo, taking a nature walk (in large, crowded cities you can take human nature walks instead), petting animals, going to the movies–and getting paid for it! And at the end of the day, when folks come to pick up their inner kids, you can tell them what their inner child did all day.

I see great financial success for this venture. I have it on good authority that in the very near future, inner child care will become tax deductible. My inner tax attorney told me so.

If Nothing Works–Do Nothing!

What if I told you you could do nothing all day and become fabulously wealthy in the process? If you say, "No way!" I say, "Absolutely right." Because now, thanks to my new network marketing company, NoWay, you can make a fortune selling boxes of Nothing. I want you to think about all those people who told you that nothing could make you rich and successful. Well, here is your chance to prove them right!

I tell you, this is a business opportunity whose time has come, because no matter what your problem is, Nothing will help. For example, Nothing has been proven to cure every disease imaginable. That's right. Studies show that placebos alone are effective in about 20 percent of cases–and what better placebo than Nothing? You can forget about pesky product liability lawsuits. We promise Nothing–and we deliver. How many companies can make that claim?

Imagine how refreshing it will be for your friends who have been inundated with multilevel marketing opportunities. You can truthfully tell them you have Nothing to sell–and then sell it to them! Yes, in a world filled with products that are really nothing disguised as something, you can sell something disguised as Nothing. Think of all those pessimystics out there who insist that nothing can help the starving multitudes, nothing can alleviate poverty, nothing can revive our neighborless 'hoods. I say, let's prove them right and prove them wrong at the same time. Imagine armies of homeless or unemployed young folks selling boxes of Nothing door-to-door. "They told me nothing could get me off the streets," they might say, "and I am hoping they are right. Will you help?"

Now why, you might ask, would anyone be interested in buying Nothing? Well, for one thing, most of us already have everything. In fact, we have so much of everything that we can't appreciate nothing. After all, God made the entire Universe from nothing. And the same holds true of our own creations. Every painting begins with an empty canvas, every book with a blank page, every symphony with silence to be filled. As Harry Cohen Baba used to say, "Listen, if you don't know Nothing, you don't know nothing."

Of course, being a FUNdamentalist, I couldn't resist putting some funny jokes about nothing on the box. This is a perfect product for those diagnosed with humorrhoids and who insist, "Nothing makes me laugh." So not only will you be striking a blow for the invisible nothing in a world cluttered with visible somethings, but you will be raising the laugh force on the planet- and creating a mannafestival of the first order. Imagine millions and millions of people all around the globe being fed and prospered by Nothing. Now that's what I call manifesting manna!

Another Zen Cohen

A visitor to Harry Cohen Baba's ashram once complained to the Garment Centered One about the use of certain herbal laughsitives around the ashram. Whereupon Harry offered the following parable. Two seminary students shared the same vice: smoking cigarettes. Plagued by guilt, they decided each to go separately to the Monsignor and ask permission to smoke. When next they saw each other and compared notes, they were puzzled to find they had each been given a different answer.

"I asked the Monsignor if I could smoke while I was praying," said the first student, "and he said, 'Certainly not!'"

"That's funny," said the second. "I asked if it was all right if I prayed while I was smoking, and he said, 'Of course.'"

What? You Still Have Questions?

Dear Swami:
I've been hearing a lot lately about the power of visualization to manifest more of what you want in life. It seems pretty amazing that I can sit in my room, focus my mind and imagine something, and then have it come

about. Can anyone learn to do this? Does it really work?

Lil Bitmore
Asheville, North Carolina

Dear Lil:

Yes, it is true. Visualization is indeed a powerful tool. And unless you suffer from a serious yearning disability, it is fairly easy to do. Does it work? Absolutely! I'll give you an example. Recently, the organizer of one of my personal appearances used this technique as a major form of promotion. Each morning for two weeks, this person would meditate for half an hour and imagine a full house for the event. And each day, the visualization became more and more vivid. Finally, the evening of the engagement arrived, and it was apparent that this imagining technique worked exquisitely. The concert hall was completely filled with imaginary people.

Dear Swami:
I have long dreamed of following my bliss and playing music full time–becoming a traveling minstrel who brings joy and celebration wherever I go. Finally, last year I sold my house and bought an RV. I was all set to go, but all of a sudden I was paralyzed with terror. Each time I try to leave, the fear returns. Now my self-esteem has suffered and I feel like such a failure. Any advice for me, Swami?

Juana Cruz
Boulder, Colorado

Dear Juana:

You are not the first would-be traveling musician who has fallen victim to pre-minstrel syndrome. Fortunately, a healthy infusion of esteem will help cure your periodic affliction. Find yourself a good esteem room to play in, and soak in that esteem. If you must acknowledge a failure, give yourself credit (even if your creditors won't). Never call yourself a failure. Instead, stand tall and proudly say, "When it comes to failing, I am tremendously successful!" Become your own esteem generator, and you'll never be bothered by minstrel cramping again.

> Dear Swami:
> I've been building up some terrific karmic debts this lifetime, and all I can say is, I hope the Universe's interest rate is lower than the one I'm paying on my condo. I'll be blunt, Swami. Is there any way to negotiate this? After all the high-rolling this time around, I don't think I can handle a lower birth.
>
> *Upton O. Goode*
> *Las Vegas, Nevada*

Dear Upton:

Well, you do have a few choices. You could declare moral bankruptcy, and try to cut a deal with the Eternal Revenue Service. A good universal lawyer could probably get you off with about three thousand years of community service. Or, you can do one of those consolidation loans for your karmic debts. You've heard of Evelyn Wood's speed reading course? Well, I offer Swami Beyondananda's Speed Suffering. That is where we cram eons worth of suffering into one miserable week. Believe me, it will be insufferable! But hey, when you're done you'll have no more karma payments, and you'll own your life free and clear. Personally, my suggestion is for you to stop running up all that karmic debt, and start paying it back, however slowly. You know that Karmic Relief benefit they have every year? If I were you, I would start donating some good deeds to those less fortunate. (You might even want to start by donating the deed to your condo.) And don't be concerned with getting a lower birth. Upper birth, lower birth–it makes no difference. We all pull into the station at the same time.

Dear Swami:
I understand you have learned the secret for making a small fortune in the stock market. Can you share it with us?

Bill Yanaire
Hilton Head, South Carolina

Dear Bill:
Yes. Start with a large fortune.

Dear Swami:
I thought I heard on the radio the other day that overall crime is down compared with fifty years ago. As a resident of the 'hood, I see crime increasing all the time. What do you think, Swami? Is overall crime really down? And what can be done to make the 'hood a less dangerous place?

Amos B. Haven
Los Angeles, California

Dear Amos:
The radio report was absolutely right. Overall crime is down compared to fifty years ago. In 1950, for example, some 30 percent of all crime was committed by people in overalls. Today, that figure is just under 8 percent. As for the 'hood, I agree it is more deadly than ever before. And I think this deadly 'hood is due to lack of livelihood. Unfortunately, when the most profitable forms of livelihood in the 'hood are deadly, only the deadly hoods have a livelihood. So how do we fix this problem? Well, when we take a look under the hood, we see that what we now call the "'hood" used to be called the "neighborhood." This tells me that when the "neighbor" is removed, only the "'hood" remains. So the answer is simple (although it may not be easy). If we want to turn a deadly 'hood into a lively 'hood, the neighbors must be stronger in force than the hoods–and the promise of livelihood must be greater than the profits of deadlihood.

Dear Swami:
I am a body-worker who has a thriving practice. And yet, I feel dissatisfied because there are so many people out there who are suffering with stress and tension, and who don't even know my services are available. I'd like to do some outreach work, but I'm not sure how. Any ideas?

Carol Ott
Tiburon, California

Dear Carol:

It is heartening to see someone into self-development who actually wants to do something to help the working stiff. Obviously, you haven't heard of Feels on Wheels, the organization dedicated to bringing healing massage to those who are hopelessly out of touch. Their philosophy is simple: "Some need to be kneaded; some need to knead to be needed. Those needing kneading are kneadless needlessly as long as we heed the need to knead the needy." Best of luck working with the have-knots.

Swami's Omwork Assignment:

How To Attune Your Own Karma

As someone who's been working on karmas for years, I will tell you that fixing your karma is easier than you might think. Sure, you might have to see Mr. Godwrench for your twenty thousand-year check up, but most problems you can fix yourself by learning these simple Auto Suggestion Techniques. Say goodbye to invasive mechanical procedures and harmful engine additives, and you will get better smileage (and we all know how important smileage is when it comes to your karma).

Use this healing relaxation at the first sign of karma trouble:

- Put your karma into park.
- Turn off your ignition.
- Let your weight sink slowly into your tires.
- Let your shock absorbers release all the tensions of the road.
- Let all exhaustion escape from your tailpipe.

Drive Your Karma, Curb Your Dogma

Good. Now repeat the following affirmations as you breathe deeply through your intake mannafold:

- "My battery is fully charged and I am getting plenty of juice."
- "My transmission is engaged, and my karma has shifted into overdrive."
- "My front end is aligned with perfection."
- "I am at One with my Universal Joint."
- "I cruise easily with the flow of traffic, and experience no delays."
- "I get off at the mannafestival."

May your karma run smoothly until it is recalled by the Maker. Oh, and don't forget to leave your dogma at home.

Part IV

Milk The Sacred Cow—And Take The Bull By The Horns

When You See A Sacred Cow... Milk It For All It's Worth

You have only to turn on your TV or take a look at the tabloids these days to see that the sacred cow has become an endangered species. Yes, it seems that everyone has an ox to grind nowadays. Whether it's the Prince's private conversations or the President's private privates, nothing escapes the cultural meat-grinder. And I have to tell you, I've got a beef with that. Personally, I think that if we just milked the sacred cow and laughed at the bull, we wouldn't need to resort to such butchery.

But the first time Harry Cohen Baba spoke to me about milking the sacred cow and taking the bull by the horns, I must admit I had no idea what he was talking about. "Why do we need these sacred cows anyway?" I asked him. "Don't they just wander aimlessly in the streets and slow down traffic? Those sacred cows could feed a lot of people, you know."

"First of all," he answered, "I happen to think that we've reached the point in this so-called civilization where anything that wanders aimlessly and slows down traffic is a good thing. Secondly, those sacred cows do feed a lot of people. You've heard the expression 'the milk of human kindness?' Where do you think it comes from? Sacred cows bring us spiritual food directly from the Fodder. I'm telling you, when we slaughter the sacred cow, we are killing the golden goose."

"But where does the bull fit in?" I asked.

"If you mean literally," he replied, "that is strictly between the bull and the cow. If you mean figuratively, I will explain. In the beginning, we humans just let Spirit nourish us in its Motherly way and we lived in Udder Bliss. But somewhere along the line, someone figured out that the head was good for something other than cracking coconuts. We started thinking, which is OK, and then we starting thinking a lot, which is problematic. And somewhere, I think it was back there during the Age of Taurus, the sacred cow got overrun by the bull. It is no accident, by the way, that churchly decrees used to be called Papal Bulls."

"Now wait a minute," I protested. "Don't you think some folks might take that last statement as a Papal smear and be offended?"

"Why should they?" the Garment Centered One replied. "Certainly, Jesus showed us the whey. But you know how people are. Instead of doing the milking and extracting the cream themselves, they get lazy and would rather be formula-fed. After generations of this pasteurized, homogenized, two percent spirituality, the body politic has lapsed into a deep cattlepsy. And without this direct connection to the Fodder, we've allowed a powerful few to bulldoze Mother Nature and seek immortality in their own creations." He paused to poke me in the ribs with his kosher dill. "And that's why the sacred cow is nowhere to be found, but the bull is everywhere."

This was beginning to make sense. But I still didn't understand how exactly we milked the sacred cow. "How exactly do we milk the sacred cow?" I asked.

"By laughing at God," the Garment Center Saint replied.

"Laughing at God?" I gasped. "That sounds like a blasphemy!"

"Of course it is!" he said, thumping me on the back. "It's a blast for you, it's a blast for me, it's a blast for everybody! And it's a blast for God. Ever since Adam first tripped on one of Eve's discarded banana peels, the Creator has been laughing at us. He has gotten countless laughs at our expense, and I think the only thing that may have dampened His laughter a little bit is that we haven't completely joined in the fun."

"But laughing at God...," I protested. "It's sounds so disrespectful."

"Nah," he scoffed. "Not laughing at God is what's disrespectful. If God is laughing, who are we not to laugh? Besides, when we don't milk our sacred cows by extracting every drop of joy and laughter from them, they wither and dry-and then what good are they? That is why so many poor souls have been turning away from the Fodder, and seeking nourishment from the bull."

I was beginning to see his point. "OK, just how do we laugh at God?"

"Well," he said, "God is everywhere and God is everything, right? So laughing at God means laughing at everything everywhere."

"Wait a minute," I said. "Do you mean to say we should laugh at tragedy? That sounds hurtful to me."

"Not if you realize that from the Creator's perspective, tragedy is temporary but joy is everlasting. Wasn't that what the Resurrection was about?"

"So I should laugh at funerals?" I persisted.

"Why not? We FUNdamentalists do it all the time," he said. "Instead of a wake, we have a roast. We remember and repeat all the funny things that person did and said, because we know that one of the first things that happens when you reach the next world is they have a big roast for you with all of your friends over there. Haven't you ever heard that FUNdamentalist blessing, 'You should only roast in heaven?'"

"OK," I said. "But what if other people are in pain? Do we just laugh in their faces?"

"Of course not!" said Harry Cohen Baba. "That would be cruel. The polite thing would be to laugh behind their backs instead. But we already spend enough time and energy doing that. If you really want to milk the sacred cow for laughs, you gotta mine your own business. Believe me, each of us has a such a goldmine of material in our own lives, that it's enough to keep us laughing until the sacred cows come home."

"And that's milking the sacred cow?" I asked.

"Yes," said my teacher, "and one more thing. We have to

laugh the loudest and hardest at our own pet beliefs. I mean if you're going to keep the family dogma around, you may as well have fun playing with it, right?" I couldn't argue with this impeccable logic. He continued, "Behind every sacred cow there is some bull lurking in the shadows. When we learn to distinguish between the two, we can be nourished by the sacred cow without getting overrun by the bull."

"Okay," I said to him. "How exactly do I separate the cow from the bull?"

"It isn't easy," he said. "There's an old saying, 'Being able to separate the cow from the bull is what separates the men from the boys.' So I'll give you a tip. Everything we encounter in life-everything-has some nourishment and some bull. A healthy skeptic system can help us distinguish between that which is of the Fodder and that which is not."

"Yes," I persisted, "but how do we learn to make that distinction?"

"By laughing!" he said. "When we shine the light of laughter on our sacred cows, we automatically expose the bull." And he told me the following parable:

"In a small East Texas town a century ago, the town madam approached the local minister. 'Reverend,' she said, 'I would like to make amends for my life and donate everything I have to build a new chapel.'

'I need to think about it,' the minister told her. 'Please come back tomorrow.'

The next day she returned, and the minister had made his decision. 'I'm sorry,' he told her. 'I cannot accept.'

The woman left, and one of the townspeople, who had been listening in, approached the minister. 'Reverend,' said the man, 'with all due respect, we need a new building. Why did you turn down the woman's generous offer?'

'Because her money,' proclaimed the minister, 'is tainted money.'

'What are you talking about, her money?' The man replied. 'It's OUR money.'"

Taking the Bull by the Horns

The time has come to take the bull by the horns and tell it just like it is. This tone may sound a bit serious to you, but hey, our sensibilities are being trampled by some serious bull out there. So here goes. Our sacred cows have been ground into hamburger, and it seems the only thing left is profane bull. You have only to turn on the TV or take a look at the tabloids to see what I mean. The cattle industry may have taken a few cuts, but the bull industry is thriving. Not only is there more bull out there than ever before, but there is more bull about bull. (And the fact that I am writing this would indicate there is more bull about bull about bull.) In and of itself, bull is fine. I'm proud of my own B.S. degree. But when it starts to choke off the good stuff, well it's time to unclog our collective skeptic system.

Now you might be saying to yourself, "My goodness, the Swami certainly sounds cynical and disillusioned." (Or, you might be saying to yourself, "Who does that Swami think he is, putting words in my mouth?") I am here to tell you that the prime cause of disillusionment is illusionment, so if I can help disabuse you of your illusionment, perhaps it will keep you from being abused by your disillusionment. Let's start with political bull because the two words are almost interchangeable. All we hear nowadays is, "Cut spending, cut spending, cut spending!" I say, cut the bull. If we cut the bull, I guarantee the spending will plummet. Because so much of the spending is on bull. The same with our Gross National Product. Have you ever stopped to think how little of the Gross National Product is spent on nourishment and how much of it is spent on bull? I have, and it's gross. And what about the stock market? What do you think fuels the bull market? Bull, that's what! And even more bull is predicted for the future, which is why the bull market is so bullish on bull.

Now that I have shown you the negative picture, I want to turn off the TV for a moment and tell-a-vision instead. Because I have a dream. I have a dream that sometime in the very near future a talented inventor will manufacture what is perhaps the most feared weapon known to civilized man–a foolproof B.S. detector. In my dream, it is being readied for mass-production under the trade name "Truth or Consequences," and will feature a Beulah-like buzzer just like on that old TV show. When the buzzer goes "burp-BU-RRR-P!" the user will know that whoever or whatever it is being pointed at is full of you-know-what. While this devastating weapon will have the power to destroy such established icons as daytime TV, the legal profession, the advertising industry, academia, not to mention our current political system, it will pose no real harm to human life. In my dream, it is the exact opposite of the neutron bomb. Institutions will crumble, but people will be left standing.

Well, this device I dream about may or may not be invented. So in the meantime, I have another dream–that we each learn to use our own God-given skeptic system to do the job. The good news is that all this bull I've been rambling on about is the richest source of irony on the planet. As FUNdamentalists and Fu Ling practitioners, we have the happy task of absorbing these ironies and using them to neutralize all of the toxic bull inundating us. I look forward to the day when even the biggest piece of bull can be broken down into joyful laughter and harmless jokes that actually improve the atmosphere.

A word About Sects

Mention a sacred cow and its companion bull, and the topic of sects inevitably comes up. Now I don't mean to brag, but when it comes to sects I've got plenty of experience. In fact, I am a recovering sects addict. It all goes back to my dysFUNsional upbringing. In my family, laughter was frowned upon. In fact, everything was frowned upon. Consequently, there was a lot of frowning. I'll never forget the day my mother unexpectedly came into my room and caught me amusing myself. She told me in no uncertain terms that frivolous ejoculation would dissipate my laugh force. So I learned to control my urges and practice strict mirth control.

But an unhappy child is often a defiant one, and I was no exception. Ours was a Methodist family (actually my father was Methodist and my mother was Catholic, so technically I was a Rhythm-Methodist), and contact with the opposite sects was strongly discouraged. So I rebelled. As soon as I was old enough to drive my own karma, I went out cruising for sects. I became infatuated with an Oklahoma swami who called himself the Yogi from Muskogee (I have since inherited this title). I first met him when he did a yoga demonstration for my boy scout troop, and taught us how to tie ourselves into twelve different knots. I quickly embraced the path of the yogi and mastered many advanced techniques, including levitation. In fact, one of my favorite pranks in high school was to hover over the stands at football games and moon the crowd. I was the only student in the history of our high school ever to get suspended for being suspended.

Yes, I foolishly thought I was above reproach, but I got my come-downance soon after. My accelerated path to yogihood hit a dead end when my kundalini exploded in a crowded department store. No one else was injured, but I caught an inflection and was left with a permanent East Indian accent.

Now this was the late '60s, right in the midst of the Sectual Revolution, and I began to explore all kinds of kinky sects. For a while, I studied with the guru of rock 'n roll, Baba Oom Mow Mow, who taught his own version of the Golden Rule: "Do wop unto others as you would have them do wop unto you, for every act has its ramalamafications." Although the sect promised "fun, fun, fun 'til your Daddy takes your karma away," I could get no satisfaction, and soon drifted away.

A failed romance with a singer in one of Baba Oom Mow Mow's "girl groups" left me in heartbreak hotel–and that was how I came to Elvis. Actually, he came to me. One night I was crying in the chapel, when the King Himself materialized and began singing to me, "Are you lonesome tonight?" Needless to say I was all shook up, and shortly thereafter I converted to Presleyterianism. It was one of those new "lite" religions that was popping up in those days–same satisfying flavor with less than one third the commandments. The Prophet Elvis asks only three things of his followers:

1. Love Me Tender
2. Don't Be Cruel
3. Please Surrender

The faithful believe that Elvis is King of the Whole Wide World, and that Presleyterians never die, they just Return to Sender. Almost immediately, I became a devout Presleyterian, donning my ritual sideburns every morning and doing my salute to the sun while singing "Hunka Hunka Burnin' Love." I spent a few months as a missionary with the Elvis's Witnesses (you can tell them by the rings around their necks) going door-to-door presleytizing. I even made a pilgrimage to the Shrine of the Velvet Elvis in Toledo and saw the remarkable sight that many have spoken of but few have seen. As I stood looking at the King, his upper lip curled into a peaceful smile, for a moment I experienced Graceland.

Still, happiness eluded me, and I sought out wilder and wilder sects. I was addicted to Spirit, and was hitting the Source pretty hard in those days. The turning point came when I woke up one morning with a sugar hangover in a strange biker crash pad where the inhabitants wore saffron leather vests and reeked of incense. Slowly, the horrible truth dawned on me. I had become a Harley Krishna. It was then that I swore off promiscuous sects activities forever.

So what about it? Is indulging in sects good for us, or will it actually stunt our spiritual growth? My attitude is, sects between consenting adults is fine, as long as you're not obsessed with it. You see those folks who sic their dogma on anyone whose sects preference is different from their own–one look in their eyes will tell you they will do anything for sects. Let's face it, unbridled sects can lead to unwanted misconceptions, and goodness knows we already have enough of these in the world.

So how do we distinguish between good and bad sects? Well, personally, I try to avoid sects in which people are tied up, tied down, beaten up, or beaten down. I'm a great believer in sects equality, so I would be cautious of any sects involving domination. On the positive side, I would go for lots and lots of joyful and complete ejoculation. Laughter is a natural and necessary element of good sects, so if people aren't ejoculating, I would be wary. Go ahead and enjoy the wild sects but remember, just because someone finds your ch'i spot doesn't mean they have your best interests at heart. So bring protection, and no matter how ecstatic you get, be sure to keep your eyes open.

Don't Get Even–Get Odd!

Being odd is natural. Each of us is a one-of-a-kind, and number-wise, it doesn't get any odder than one. To paraphrase the old song, one is the oddest number that you'll ever do. So each of us is as odd as they come. Now of course, people do pair up–no doubt to get even. But even after getting even, we're still looking to go one-up on each other. Life is odd that way. Nobody is ever really even, except for maybe Siamese twins–and even they would prefer to get odd.

Harry Cohen Baba used to tell me all the time, "Don't get even–get odd," and it was confusing to me. One day, I said to him, "Garment Centered One, ever since I first got involved with kinky sects back in the early '70s, I've been pretty odd. In fact, my adult life has been a regular oddyssey, going from one odd adventure to another. As far as I can see, I'm already odd."

"Tell me," he said, "when you were a Presleyterian or a Harley Krishna, what did your parents think about it?"

"Oh, they were horrified."

"And how did that make you feel?"

"To be honest, I got great pleasure from it," I confessed.

"Well then," he said conclusively, "you were just getting odd to get even, weren't you?"

I had to admit he was right.

"Listen," he said, "once you realize you are driving a custom-built karma on an expressway of your own design, and you appreciate how odd you truly are, you'll lose all desire to get even. And you will be creating an alter native reality."

I corrected him. "You mean alternative reality, don't you?"

"No," he said. "I mean alter native reality. Have you been out on the streets lately and taken a look at the natives? I think their reality could use some altering, don't you?"

Indeed, just the day before I had noticed how many people in New York looked as if they had spent a good part of their lives posing for Mt. Rushmore.

He continued, this time poking me in the chest. "Listen, all these years as a tailor, don't you think I know something about alterations? And if the natives are going to be altered, they need others out there to help them milk the cow, cut the bull, and find out what fits for them. This is serious, *boychick*. Our society is dying of consumption and our children are being malled to death. And it is the job of the Fu Ling master to help bring about an alter native reality by stirring the laughingstock."

Creating An Alter-Native Reality

Do we really create our own reality? Or is it all scripted out over at Universal Studios? The debate has raged for as long as debates have been the rage, and I can provide no definitive answer either. Certainly some really big blockbusters have come out of Universal recently–and more disasteroid scenarios are predicted for the near future. And yet, small independents continue to write and star in their own successful movies.

As more and more of these alternative scripts get produced, this is helping to bring about an alter native reality. And that is a good thing, because the reality we have today is quickly losing popularity. In a recent reality check, 71 percent of those responding said they "disapproved" of current reality–the lowest approval rating reality has had since the Great Flood. This is understandable. Consider the political scene, for goodness sakes. All those endless buttals and rebuttals. The media baits us into arguing, and we keep falling for debate. It is so silly–we could be making a beautiful brainchild together, and instead we are mass-debating.

Even those natives who ignore the political goings on, they too are in need of altering. Perhaps you are one of those going through a mid-laugh crisis or mannapause and are complaining, "I seem to have outgrown my life and nothing fits anymore." Well, as Harry Cohen Baba used to say, "When something doesn't fit, what better time to make alterations?"

Now in the old days when Harry Cohen Baba was still

on the physical plane, people would come in for alterations all the time. "Your life is too tight," he would often tell them. "You need to let out some material." And he would tell them a Zen Cohen to help them do just that. Invariably, the natives would leave in a truly altered state, often remarking about how well their life fit. "Wow. No crimping in the crotch. No more constriction around the neck. And look-my arms are swinging freely!" I tell you, it was quite a blessing to have a guru who could custom-tailor your reality like that. I remember shortly before his passing, the great healer's disciples gathered at his bedside and cried, "What will we do without you?"

The Garment Centered One shrugged and said, "Suit yourself."

And this is only fitting. We can alter our own reality–not to mention the reality of the natives around us–by following these simple suggestions:

1. Make A Fool of Yourself
2. Tell-A-Vision.
3. Be An Esteem-Generator
4. Commit Random Acts of Comedy and Beautiful Nonsense

Make a Fool of Yourself

In case it hasn't become clear to you by now, we are all fools. The wise fool knows this, and takes fool advantage of the situation. The sooner we see our situation from a God's-eye-view, the sooner we laugh. The sooner we laugh, the better we feel. The better we feel, the heartier we laugh. The heartier we laugh, the easier it is to see things from God's perspective. And we've come fool circle.

By all means, encourage others to laugh at your expense. According to a recent report issued by the Eternal Revenue Service, each time someone laughs at our expense, it is credited to our Ascended Mastercard, which makes it an excellent way to buy down karmic debt. So next time you are feeling foolish; smile, shrug, and say, "This one's on me!" Who knows? You might be able to skip a few karma payments. For indeed, laughter provides karmic relief. As the old saying goes, "Laugh at yourself, and the whole world will laugh at you too." Imagine a world of fooly-realized beings wholeheartedly laughing at themselves. This would surely alter our native reality for the better.

Tell-A-Vision

Everywhere you go, it seems, you hear people complaining about their reality. I say, if you don't like the current programming, step out from behind the remote. It's time to change the channel and tell a vision. Instead of being just another divisionary taking sides on the latest televised drama, become a visionary who uses the spectacle to help us all see more clearly. If enough of us do this, even the mainstream media will have to replace its commentators with uncommontaters who have an alter native vision. For indeed there is a Divine Order. When you tell your vision, you are filling out a Divine Order Form. As Harry Cohen Baba used to say, "Life is like a good deli. If enough people order something, they'll have to make it."

One of my own visions involves the healing of one of the most tragic problems facing contemporary society–art failure. FUNdamentalists tell us the artist's purpose is to circulate life-giving ideas through the body politic. Sadly, many artists nowadays are suffering from truth decay, and as a result have become disartened. Being disartened, they can only create art that disses art–you know, the kind where people looking at it are puzzled and say, "Dis is art?"

We can cure art disease by creating and supporting heartful art–and encouraging everyone to find their own expressway. So rejoice that you are unique–just like everyone else–and remind everyone you see that they are odd as well. If we support others in being themselves, truly the odds will be with us as we promote alter native lifestyles. For it is written that on Nonjudgment Day, we will realize we are all equally odd–and that makes us even.

Be An Esteem-Generator

With the upcoming karma shift that has been predicted, we can look forward to a lot more karmas cruising the expressways. And if we want these karmas to burn as cleanly as possible, we're going to have to generate a lot of esteem. Each of us at some time in our lives has been flattened by an esteem-roller, and it's taken us months or years to get back up to a full head of esteem. You can speed up this process–and alter native reality–by becoming an empowerhouse who helps others generate their own esteem. As you know, esteem rises, and rising esteem might be behind all of this global warming we've heard so much about. People are definitely becoming warmer. Just a few years ago, it wasn't cool to be warm. Now being warm is becoming cool again. This is bound to have an effect on the overall climate.

Commit Random Acts of Comedy and Beautiful Nonsense

Many years ago when I was working odd jobs (being odd made me especially suited for this work), I was feeling stressed and depressed. As I walked along a downtown street one day, I was puzzled to find mysterious white cartoon faces painted on the sidewalk all up and down the street. I wondered who had painted these silly faces and why. That night when the street lamps came on, the mystery was solved. The light shining on the parking meters cast a shadow–and the shadows cast by the parking meters put a pair of black Mickey Mouse ears on all the white cartoon faces. Thanks to this random act of comedy, I burst out laughing and saw delight.

Have you ever had the feeling that God is toying with us

and nothing makes sense? I remember one of my last conversations with Harry Cohen Baba. I had just gone through a few days where everything I did turned out the opposite of what I'd planned. I was in the middle of a Tantrum yoga session, and in the heat of anger I accidentally set off the smoke alarm. Harry came hobbling in and asked what was wrong.

"God is toying with me," I snapped, "and nothing makes sense!"

"You're absolutely right," said the Garment Centered One.

"I know I'm right," I replied, still fuming. "So what do I do?"

"If God is toying with you," he said gently, "you can still choose to become a creative plaything. Just get out on the expressway and follow your art. As for nothing making sense, there is one thing that makes sense."

"What's that?" I asked.

"Nonsense," he replied. "We live in a society that is a slave to logic, yet look how illogical we are. We have the firepower to destroy the world twenty times over–but we haven't the resources to feed or educate the world's children. Does that makes sense? So in a world where making sense makes no sense the only thing that makes sense is nonsense!" He looked at me with a twinkle in his eye and asked, "Now doesn't that make sense?"

I have taken that advice to heart and I now pass it on to you. Each day, try to create a harmless, playful bit of nonsense that causes ripples of laughter and increases everyone's sillium level. The day will come when your clown chakra awakens, and you realize that making nonsense makes more sense than making sense. That day, you will have found the way of the Fu Ling master. And your life will be Duck Soup.

A Zen Cohen

A reporter once came to interview Albert Einstein. When she arrived at his laboratory at Princeton, she was surprised to notice a horseshoe hanging above the door.

"Professor Einstein," she said, "surely a great scientist like you doesn't believe a horse-shoe will bring good luck."

"Of course not," he replied. "I think that notion is utter nonsense."

"Then, why is that horseshoe up there?" she asked.

"Because it works whether you believe it or not," Einstein replied.

I Never Metaphysical Question I Didn't Like

> Dear Swami:
> I've heard that you actually have the ability to walk on water. Not only that, but you say you can teach others to do this as well. Where can I sign up?
>
> *Stan Doffisch*
> *Rockville, Maryland*

Dear Stan:

You heard right. Like anything else in life, walking on water is quite simple as long as the conditions are right and your timing is impeccable. So I invite all of you to join me for my annual Water Walking Ceremony on Lake Minnetonka, Minnesota, on January 15. Success is virtually guaranteed.

> Dear Swami:
> I have asked this question of many great masters, and none could answer it to my satisfaction. So I will ask you: How do you know you know?
>
> *Ashir Dropov*
> *Brooklyn, New York*

Dear Ashir:

As far as I know, there are Four Stages of Knowing:

1. You don't know.
2. You don't know you don't know.
3. You know you don't know.
4. You know "I don't know" is all you need to know.

Clearly, you have not achieved Stage Four because you still think you need to know if you know, and your desire to be aware of what you know and what you don't know has led you to a state of mental confusion. I understand this condition from my own experience because I too was a know-aware man. But then in an instant, enlightening struck and I went from know awareness to no awareness. As soon as I knew I didn't know, I knew. Y'know?

> Dear Swami:
> I wonder if other people have this problem. Every time I sit down to meditate, I am distracted by what my Catholic school teachers used to call "impure thoughts." The result is that I feel guilty, and I rededicate myself to spiritual purity—and then the cycle begins all over again.

Is there any way to end the battle between these higher states and lower states?

Dickson Frundt
Baltimore, Maryland

Dear Dickson:

Boy, it is hard to believe that after all these years, we are still fighting the War Between the States. It begins when we decide we want to do away with slavery to our passions, which is fine. There is nothing good about being enslaved. The trouble comes when our inner abolitionist decides that all passion should be abolished, and we should dwell only in the higher states. When that happens, it is natural for the lower states to rebel. So each time we try to elevate to the rarefied air of Minnesota, there is the proverbial "uprising in the south" and we get this hot sultry feeling from New Orleans all the way down to the tip of Florida. So what is the solution? Sure, you can live in a border state if you choose, and stay close to the Mason-Dixon Line of consciousness. But walking a line like that can make life—well, flat. I suggest you set up dual residences because there is a time to go north, and a time to go south. When you feel at home in both the higher states and the lower states, you truly have achieved a more perfect Union.

Dear Swami:

I have been hearing stories for years that you were once a Marxist. I find it hard to believe that someone who calls himself a FUNdamentalist once embraced Marxism. Is there any truth to this, or is it just an idle rumor?

José Cañusi
Coconut Grove, Florida

Dear José:

Well, obviously it is no idle rumor since it managed to travel to Coconut Grove. And, as a matter of fact, it is true. As part of my early comic-kaze training, I joined a Marxist study group and became adept at all three branches of

Marxism–Groucho, Chico, and Harpo Marxism. From the Groucho school of Marxism, I learned to throw rapid-fire punchlines and hurl barbs that go straight to the heart of the matter. From Chico, I learned dialectic materialism. He did all his material in dialect, you know. From Harpo Marxism, I learned to transmute. That is where you magically transform tension into laughter without saying a word. If you ask me, the Harpos are the most subversive Marxists of all. Since they never say anything, they can never be silenced.

> Dear Swami:
> Can you explain the Theory of Relativity?
> *Gordy Yinnott*
> *Mill Valley, California*

Dear Gordy:

Sure. A billionaire comes down to breakfast one morning and tells his wife he feels like a million bucks. She says, "Oh my goodness. What's wrong?"

> Dear Swami:
> I've been hearing a lot lately about "New Thought." What exactly is New Thought, and how does it differ from Old Thought?
> *Waylon Wahl*
> *Tulsa, Oklahoma*

Dear Waylon:

The Old Thought governing belief is: Bread always falls buttered side down. New Thought maintains that bread always falls buttered side up, and if by some quirk your bread falls buttered side down, you obviously buttered the wrong side.

> Dear Swami:
> How do you feel about sage-burning for purification purposes?
> *Al Lurgic,*
> *King of Prussia, Pennsylvania*

Dear Al:

True, there are some today who would like to restore that medieval practice, but I think it would be counterproductive. Sages have always been an endangered species and, particularly these days, we need every sage we can get!

> Dear Swami:
>
> I'm mad as hell and I'm not gonna take it anymore! Ever since I was a child, I've been told that if I was good and said my prayers and so on, that God's blessings would rain down on me. Any adversity, I was told, would be blessings in disguise. Well, let me tell you, my blessings have been so disguised that they're virtually unrecognizable. Not a day goes by that the bluebird of happiness doesn't drop a juicy one on my new suit. On top of that, some psychic told me the other day that I actually chose everything that happens in my life! Before I was born I made a contract with God and I agreed to have all these "lessons." Well, I must have been the victim of false advertising, because I know I didn't ask for this. Swami, you know about these things. Is there any way I can get out of the contract?
>
> *Ike Witt*
> *Flushing, New York*

Dear Ike:

It's obvious you got a lousy deal. If I were you, I'd get myself an attorney who has argued in front of the real Supreme Court, and I'd sue. It's already being done by others, so why shouldn't you give it a shot? I've read several articles lately from all across the country where people who feel they've been misled or gotten a bum deal are suing God. Now of course, God himself carries very little cash—and you know how hard those Swiss banks are to get into. So people are doing the next best thing—suing religious organizations. I have an article right here about some guy who's suing the Catholic Church because he claims Hail Marys "simply don't work." In his deposition, he goes on to say that Hail Marys were not adequately tested before they were put out on the market, and calls the Church's miraculous claims "misleading."

So I can only encourage you to press your suit (but be sure to get the dry cleaners to remove the bird droppings first). I should warn you, however, that God uses only the best lawyers–part of an elaborate trade agreement with Satan–and the settlement could be delayed for years, centuries even. On the positive side, God has a reputation for being merciful–so there is always the chance he will hear your plaintiff cry and settle out of court.

> Dear Swami:
> I know that you've told us the slogan for the new millennium is "Shift Happens," but I must be stuck back in the old one, because the word that describes my life is "stagnation." After more than ten years of being "on the path," I feel I'm further away from enlightenment and peace of mind than when I started. I've read all the books, listened to all the tapes, gone to dozens of seminars, and instead of answers I've got more questions. I'm bewildered, Swami. Isn't there anything that can help me attain peace of mind?
>
> *Guy Dussall*
> *Mt. Shasta, California*

Dear Guy:

Your situation sounds uncomfortable, but it is far from unusual. Many people who start out seeking paradise find paradox instead, and they become so uncomfortable in their uncertainty that they'd do anything to be led out of the bewilderness. That's why so many people nowadays flock around any two-bit charlatan with an axiom to grind–and they usually end up sorry. If you're one of those sorry flockers looking for immediate relief, there is a product I can recommend. It is called Right God spray. Just spray in your general vicinity at the first sign of uncertainty, and watch doubts dissolve in minutes. And Right God's tiny little time-release dogmas will go to work instantly to keep you doubt-free for up to twelve hours—that's twice as long as Sure! And for those really, really deep-seated doubts, you can try Right God suppositories.

But actually, like most things you can buy in a drug store, Right God just deals with the symptoms. If you ask me—and you actually did—I think you're scared shiftless! Like most people who've grown up in our left-brained society, you're afraid to be in your right mind. And when you have an entire nation of people who can only rely on the logical, male side of their brains, of course we have a stag-nation. So why not open up to the intuitive female part of yourself, and have it make a doe-nation? By using each piece of your mind, you will gain peace of mind as well.

Now of course this probably sounds a lot like what you've been reading in all those books that haven't worked for you, so I will give you an exercise to do. Next time that you notice you are thinking too much (and if you are reading this, that's right now), begin by taking a deep, relaxing inhale, then let it out with a satisfying "a-a-a-ah-h-h-h!" (This is actually an ancient Vedic technique taught to me by the great master, Sigh Baba.) Do this repeatedly until your center of consciousness departs from the cold, board room atmosphere of your brain into the warm hearth of your heart. Now, take all of those decisions that you have been kicking around up there in the board room and see how they feel while you're warming yourself in the glow of love. And relax! Relax in the knowledge that you will find all answers within. Best of luck matching them with the corresponding questions.

Swami's Omwork Assignment:

The Daily Practice of Fu Ling

All indications are that in this new millennium we will need more Duck Soup than ever before. The pessimystics are making their usual dire predictions–hordes of humorless huddled outside a shabby Duck Soup kitchen waiting for a few crummy jokes. But this need not happen if we prepare enough laughingstock to last through any crisis. Remember, laughingstock stores indefinitely as long as you keep adding to it. Here is a daily practice that will keep you and everyone else laughing until the sacred cows come home:

1. *Wake Up Laughing*. It has been said the great Fu Ling masters are able to laugh at the very instant they wake up in the morning–or at least the first moment they catch a glimpse of themselves in the mirror. There's no reason why you can't do the same. If the thought of looking at yourself in the mirror first thing in the morning seems horrifying, try this: Pretend you are looking at someone else. The worse you look, the harder you will laugh. As you laugh, you will begin to look better and better until you no longer look funny enough to laugh at. When you stop laughing on your own accord, you have dispersed the laugh force throughout your body and you are ready to start the day.

2. *Mine Your Own Business.* It has been said that the bull is always funnier on the other side of the fence, but the first place to look for bull is in your own back yard. Your own bull makes the heartiest laughingstock. Every day, find something that's funny about your own laugh story and laugh at it. Laughter will help dissolve your bull. When nothing is left of the bull, you will have achieved the goal of every aspiring Fu Ling master—you will have the No Bull Peace Prize.

3. *Up Your Irony Intake.* I've upped my irony intake, up yours! When it becomes known that you are injesting ironies, people you hardly know will send you computer files filled with them. Yes, in creating a farce-field of laughter, you will become a magnet for irony filings.

4. *Humor Yourself And Others.* Practice lobbing one-liners into overly-serious conversations. When you hear an explosion of laughter, you know you hit your target. Take jokes from the Internet, share them on the Outernet. There's nothing like watching a joke detonate right in front of your eyes. If it is easier to remember short jokes, then short jokes are fine. Humorologists tell us it's not the length of the joke that matters, it's how much pleasure it gives. A good joke proliferates and nourishes like manna. Think about it. One person arrives with a good joke, and dozens leave with it!

Afterword: Love the Fun You're with

As you've probably concluded by now, life is more fun when you laugh. So love the fun you're with—even if it doesn't feel like fun at the moment. Anyone can have fun having fun. But having fun not having fun is the Fu Ling Master's art. Next time you're not having fun—and not having fun not having fun—remind yourself that life is a comedy of situations and that you're just having an episode.

If life is nothing but a sitcom, what else can you do but sit calm and enjoy it? Picture yourself as the Creator's favorite toy—a little rubber ducky sitting calm in a sea of Duck Soup. As soon as you do, you will begin to feel ripples of laughter washing over you. May you have the last laugh, and may your laughingstock last forever.

About the Author

Swami Beyondananda is the brainchild and altered ego of writer/humorist Steve Bhaerman. Steve, who spent his deformative years in Brooklyn and now resides in the Texas Hill Country, travels extensively performing as the Swami and offering his workshop on "The Alchemy of Humor." His monthly syndicated column, "Ask the Swami," is read by millions, and has been described both as "wisdom disguised as comedy" and "comedy disguised as wisdom." He is the author of *Driving Your Own Karma*, and has produced three highly-acclaimed live comedy tapes, *The Yogi From Muskogee*, *Enlightening Strikes Again*, and *Don't Squeeze the Shaman.*

Give the Gift of Laughter!